Should Mom Live With Us?

And Is Happiness Possible If She Does?

Vivian F. Carlin

Vivian E. Greenberg

LEXINGTON
BOOKS

Lexington Books

An Imprint of Macmillan, Inc.

NEW YORK

Maxwell Macmillan Canada

TORONTO

Maxwell Macmillan International

NEW YORK · OXFORD · SINGAPORE · SYDNEY

PUBLIC LIBRARY

EAST ORANGE, NEW JERSEY

Library of Congress Cataloging-in-Publication Data

Carlin, Vivian F.
Should mom live with us? : and is happiness possible if she does?
/ Vivian F. Carlin, Vivian E. Greenberg.
p.   cm.
Includes bibliographical references and index.
ISBN 0-669-28078-X
1. Mothers and daughters—United States. 2. Parent and adult
child—United States. 1. Greenberg, Vivian E.   II. Title.
HQ755.85.C357   1992   91-42598
306.874—dc20   CIP

Lexington Books
An Imprint of Macmillan, Inc.
866 Third Avenue, New York, N.Y. 10022

Maxwell Macmillan Canada, Inc.
1200 Eglinton Avenue East
Suite 200
Don Mills, Ontario M3C 3N1

Macmillan, Inc. is part of the Maxwell Communication
Group of Companies.

Printed in the United States of America

printing number
1   2   3   4   5   6   7   8   9   10

*We dedicate this book
to our husbands,
Ben and Stan.*

Contents

Introduction

Athough elderly parents and adult children have lived together through-out the centuries, in the United States this living arrangement is entered into with greater reluctance. Most older Americans prefer to maintain households separate from their children, with a recent American Association of Retired Persons (AARP) housing survey indicating that the proportion of those wanting to age in their own homes has grown.[1]

Despite this trend, adult children, in their desire to do the "right" thing, rush to invite parents to move in. Realizing only too late that they and their parents might have been better served living apart, they wish they had given the matter more thought. Few children of aging parents are aware of the many financial, house-maintenance, and safety programs that might enable a parent to remain in her own home. Few know about new research into housing arrangements that offer supportive environments to the elderly, that can meet a parent's needs for care and socialization without the sacrifice of independence and control entailed with the move into a child's home. Children, relieved of everyday responsibilities and chores, and parents, pleased not to be a burden, find their relationship strengthened rather than stressed, that living apart has brought them closer together.

For a variety of economic, social, and medical reasons, however, although elderly parents moving in with children may disrupt family harmony, this arrangement has become a realistic option for both generations. Latest statistics show that about 13 percent of older noninstitutionalized persons live with children, siblings, or other relatives. "The percentage of older persons living with their children increases with age: 14% of the men and 26% of the women over 85 years of age live with one of their children."[2]

As the costs of home health care and the fees charged by life care communities rise and as the waiting lists for apartments in senior community housing grow longer, elderly persons, though preferring to live independently, may find themselves at their children's front doors. With 23 percent of persons over sixty-five suffering from disabling ailments, the chances that the parent moving in may be chronically ill have greatly increased.[3] This living arrangement may not be the one of choice for either generation; yet, as we know, necessity creates strange bedfellows.

Additionally, as women enter the labor force in unprecedented numbers while still having responsibilities to marriage and family, they often find it easier to have Mom or Dad under the same roof than miles or even minutes away. After all, with Mom right there in Daughter's house, Daughter does not have to shop for and lug groceries to two separate residences; nor after a hard day at work does she have to run to Mother's home in the event of a sudden crisis. For the working and even nonworking daughter, it may simply be more convenient and, as a result, less physically and emotionally draining to have Mom live with her.

There are financial benefits to this arrangement as well. For the very poor or very rich in this country, procuring concrete support services (e.g., transportation, home-health aides, medical day care, nurses) poses less of an economic hardship than for those in the middle who cannot qualify for Medicaid and cannot afford to purchase such services on the open market. For those (of us) in the middle the outpouring of expenditures seems endless and may ultimately be bankrupting. Consequently, for Mom, who broke her hip and requires home health assistance and extensive physical therapy, moving in with Daughter allows her to use the money saved on montly rent for these necessary services.

For adult children who find themselves dipping into their own pockets to help an elderly parent make ends meet, having Mom or Dad move in is a sensible way to cut costs. With Mom or Dad under the same roof, the drain lessens. According to a recent Gallup Poll, *The Family in America,* three adult children in ten say they helped a parent financially in the past year. The figure increases to 36 percent among children age 50 and over.[4]

Consider too the social benefits for Mom when she moves in with Daughter. Living alone, with her social network depleted by the loss of cherished friends, Mom's existence is lonely and depressing. Living in Daughter's house with Daughter's family ends her isolation. She knows that even if Daughter works, when the day is over, they will at least sit down to dinner together. Mom will again be part of a family and, if she is in good health, may even play an active role in the household. Moreover, the long hours of fitful sleep common to most elderly seem less agonizing when Mom knows there is someone sleeping in a nearby room. Fearful of being without anyone who really cares should accident or illness strike, Mom knows Daughter will be there for her. The parent who moves in has a sense of security and comfort that cannot be provided by an institution.

Aside from economic, social, and medical factors that compel elderly parents and their adult children to share a household, some choose this option simply because it is what is expected. These parents and children have a family norm, rooted in cultural or ethnic values or in family tradition, that holds living together as the way children are supposed to care for their parents. However, in today's world where caregiver children work and parents live longer than ever with chronic ailments, children have neither the time nor energy to give the comprehensive care a frail parent may require. Ten percent of the caregivers are themselves over 65 and simply do not have the physical and emotional resources for sustained long-term care.

Daughters and their elderly mothers are the protagonists in the shared household. Half of all older women in 1989 were widows, and there were five times as many widows as widowers. Sons, as well, though less frequently, may find it necessary to have Mom or Dad move in, in which case their wives (daughters-in-law) assume the major portion of caregiving chores. The research of Amy Horowitz and other gerontology scholars confirms that daughters-in-law are the primary caregivers when their husbands are called upon to take in an aging parent.[5] Indeed, our culture traditionally expects females to be the caregivers in our society. Despite efforts by the women's movement to equalize irrational gender differences, caregiving, like housekeeping, is still women's work. Thus, when Mom moves into Son's house the burden of caregiving is placed on Daughter-in-Law.

Although much has been made of another current trend relating to the return of adult children in their twenties and thirties to their parents' homes, the reverse has received little attention. Since most elderly live independently, this neglect is easy to understand. Only those involved in pertinent areas of gerontology or actually practicing this living arrangement know how this mixture of two generations under the same roof can produce tension and conflict.

When Mom moves in with Daughter, she is in all likelihood a widow who has enjoyed at least five to ten years of independence. She came and went as she wished and accounted to no one. Moving in with Daughter represents an end to her free lifestyle, for she must adjust to the rules, habits, and rhythms of another household, a household where she is not in charge. On Daughter's turf, she must close her eyes to those of Daughter's ways of which she disapproves and take a back seat to certain family matters and doings. Neither a parent in the way she once was, nor a head of household, Mom must carve out a new role for herself that will bring meaning and gratification to her life.

For Daughter, Mom's arrival can mean that her privacy will be reduced and her daily routines disrupted, and, perhaps, her lifestyle and values questioned or criticized. Suddenly, she feels like a little girl again; whereas when Mom lived apart, their relationship seemed more adult. Daughters who have been happily married report undercurrents of unease in the marital bond as their husbands voice discomfort if not outright resentment over reduced time together because of Mother's presence. Pressure rises as daughters/wives strive to meet the needs of their mothers *and* their husbands in a loving manner.

It all seemed so simple back then when Mom had a stroke and after her discharge from the hospital moved in with Daughter's family. Whoever thought that an arrangement so right and natural could be so stressful? What happened that caused things to go awry?

Both parent and child, however, forgot how the many years of separate living widen and rigidify the generation gap. At this stage in the development of parent and child, lifestyles may be the most opposite, creating a tension that makes the stormy times of adolescence seem almost blissful by comparison.

At this stage as well, the adult children have reached middle age and are ready to savor the opportunites for enjoyment and fulfillment heralded by these years. With the current divorce rate, many couples may be "remarrieds" for whom the care of elderly parents represents an intrusion into that important early stage of their new relationship. Either way, Mom's moving in will more than likely dampen, if not curtail anticipated hopes and plans.

Yet, we found shining examples of successful shared households. They are signposts clearly showing us the way to make living together mutually gratifying for all involved. Since most shared households, however, are problematic by nature, our efforts are directed to help those who are considering this arrangement make what is for them the right decision.

Since too, the right decision may entail parents and children living apart, we explore in depth the many existing programs from alternate housing arrangements to devices that enable the elderly to live safely in their own homes.

Sometimes the decision to live together, though not "right," may be the only option. In such instances, there is also help. We have found guidelines and strategies directed at reducing the strains of living together after years of living separately. We will show how to identify problems early, how to communicate openly, how to negotiate differing expectations in order to prepare both parties for what lies ahead in a way that will strengthen parent-child ties. The mere acknowledgment by parent and child that living together is inherently stressful and will require effort to make it work is a critical first step.

Contrary to popular belief, the American family is not in danger of demise. The Gallup Poll cited earier shows that family ties not only endure but strengthen as the family ages and adult children become caregivers to their parents. According to the poll, "People enjoy being with their family members and wish they had more time to spend with them." That despite a transient population, "Most adult children live within one hour's driving distance of a parent . . . and continue to stay in touch with their extended families over the course of their lifetimes."[6] Efforts, nonetheless, must be made to sustain and nourish the bonds that hold the family together. In a world growing more and more depersonalized, the family remains the final refuge where human beings can feel safe to be who they really are.

We wrote this book to preserve the family during those years when parents turn to their adult children to meet their needs. Even in the best of families, these years are stressful. Yet, they afford a final opportunity for parents and children to finish old business, erase past resentments, and get to know one another as whole human beings. With a quickening sense of mortality, both generations are eager to achieve closeness and understanding. In fact, middle-aged children, as they reasses their relationships with their parents, examine those with their own children. The relationship dynamics of one generation illuminate those of the next, as adult children strive to produce warmer connections with their children. Whatever the choice—living together or apart—it should lead to the strengthening and enrichment of the ties that bind each generation to the next.

Should Mom Live with Us?

Reasons For and Against Choosing a Shared Household

Should Mom live with us? The answer to this question is both "yes" and "no." Either response is okay and each depends upon a multiplicity of criteria. The decision to share a house among two, three, and sometimes four generations of family members is a major one, impacting significantly upon those involved and upon the way they wish to live. Whole lives can and are changed when parents and children decide to share a household. Because the decision, once made, is almost irreversible, because the changes—selling of property and house furnishings, renovations to the child's home, relocation to new and unfamiliar places—required to effect it are of considerable magnitude, its consequences must be given hard thought.

Although in Asia and parts of Western Europe, taking care of elderly parents in the home of the adult child is the norm, many elderly in this country also have this expectation. In an effort to be the "good child" implied in the parental expectation, adult children eagerly rush to fill the role. The powerful biblical injunction "to honor thy father and mother" —no matter what the personal cost or reality—only fuels the adult child's zeal. Inviting a parent to move in because it is the "right" thing to do may just work; more frequently, however, motivation colored by guilt is not a sound basis for a harmonious, mutually satisfying shared household. Such an impetus additionally strains the bond between the elder parent and the adult child.

We unequivocally reiterate: whatever decision parent and child reach is neither good nor bad. No judgment is attached to either option. Adult children, by and large, do choose to care for their elderly parents. Given the family, work, financial, and other pressures that pervade their lives, they are doing the best they can to be there for their parents during their years of dependency. Elderly parents, as well, in a world growing more and more depersonalized, turn to their children, if not for concrete support then for the affirmation that they are people worth being with and later remembered. Immortality is indeed achieved through those special family encounters where wise old heads share with younger ones anecdotes and advice that endure through the generations.

Whether filial obligation extends to having elderly parents move in with their adult children is a deeply personal matter. Every family is different in its capacity to care, its composition, its history, and whether it can tolerate the disruptions in routine and lifestyle intrinsic to the shared household. No one can self-righteously command: "You should have Mom move in with you; if you do not, you are bad." The choice is individual and must also take into account other housing options that would afford the aging parent a few more years of precious independence.

Adult children, propelled by the moral imperative to honor their parents often assume that past a certain age their parents neither wish to nor are they able to live alone. Forgetting their parents are survivors who have already "made it," they act on their own agendas of what *they* believe is in their parents' best interests. They do not credit their elders with the inner resources and strengths that have already brought them to this exalted point. Nor do they credit them with the ability to change and adapt—whether the decision is for Mom to remain in her own home or move in with her adult child. Infantilizing a parent by making choices for her is not only demeaning but robs her of whatever autonomy remains during her final years.

Children, furthermore, in their well-intentioned ardor to be "good children," do not take stock of what a major move can mean to a parent emotionally and physically. Unless parent and child already live nearby, a physical move for Mom can be heart wrenching. As if loss of home were not enough, the parent must also deal with loss of a comfortable, nurturing world, where supermarket, drugstore, post office, hairdresser, and dentist's and doctor's offices are not only known but peopled by warm and familiar faces. One can and must ask whether such a drastic move is really necessary. No matter what survival strengths a parent has, why assault her with cataclysmic changes when there may be other options?

Preserving the parent-child bond is what matters. At this stage, when both generations desire friendship and closeness, decisions that produce tension are to be avoided. The old age of parents and the middle age of their children offer a precious final opportunity for both generations to get to know one another as persons outside the restrictions of the hierarchical parent-child relationship. Whatever the decision—to live together or apart—it must foster warmth and closeness.

The following illustrate how two families came to grips with situations where moving in with children became an option. Each family is different; each family did what had to be done for its own reasons and in accordance with its own nature and limitations.

Joyce, aged eighty and divorced for forty years, lived in a large two-story, thirteen-room house in the Northeast. Fiercely independent and valuing a place of her own, Joyce always found ways to remain in her home. When her children finally left, she rented rooms to college students; when degenerative arthritis in both legs required her to use a walker, she invited Michael, a family friend who needed a place to live, to move in with her.

For twenty years Joyce and Michael lived together amicably. He was in charge of repairs and maintenance; she prepared the meals; they shared household expenses. Then Michael died suddenly of a massive coronary, leaving Joyce alone once again.

With her customary tenaciousness and determined to keep her home, Joyce enlisted the help of a young couple who had moved in next door when Michael was still alive. During these years, the two families forged a close relationship. Michael, a carpenter by trade, did the neighbor's repairs. Joyce babysat their children.

Because they felt indebted to Joyce for the help that she and Michael had given them, these neighbors happily became Joyce's caretakers after Michael's death. They did her household maintenance chores, took her marketing, shopping, and to doctors' appointments, and looked in on her every day. In return, Joyce treated the family to a dinner out at least once a week and was a substitute grandmother to the couple's two children. Had her neighbor not become pregnant with her third child, necessitating a move to a larger home, this mutually satisfying arrangement would have lasted much longer. Alone again, this time Joyce turned to her family for help.

Of Joyce's two children, only her daughter, Sally, who lived in a neighboring state was in a position to help her make long-term plans for her care. Sally assumed her new role grudgingly. She and her mother had never been close or even liked each other. Sally's husband, Tom, likewise had negative feelings for Joyce. As he put it, "Joyce was always difficult to get along with. She was never a happy person, full of regrets and bitterness, and always unpleasant to be with. I always wanted to stay as far away from her as possible. I especially did not want her underfoot all the time in my own house. Though during the years she had her housemate, she actually mellowed, and Joyce and I for the first time could tolerate a once a month visit."

Faced with the difficult decision of finding a suitable housing solution for Joyce, Sally and Tom immediately placed Joyce's home on the market and began their search. What they had not counted on, however, was the quick sale of Joyce's home, leaving Joyce no place to go except to move in with Sally and Tom.

This temporary dress rehearsal was serendipitous, in that it settled once and for all the question of whether Joyce should move in with her children. Since Sally and Tom both worked, Joyce was alone all day, without neighbors or friends to visit. Lonely and depressed, she vented her frustration at her children. Joyce had reverted to the old self that Sally and Tom found so unpleasant. In no time, the relationship deteriorated, with all three either fighting or moving around the house in total silence. Furthermore, Sally's heavy work schedule made it impossible for her to do the extra shopping, cooking, and other chores that her mother now required.

As a result of their temporary housesharing, all agreed Joyce needed a supportive living arrangement that she could afford and would be close to her daughter's home. A congregate housing development (see Chapter 4) eight miles away that expected to have a vacancy in a few months proved to be the perfect solution.

Joyce moved into her new home where she has been extremely happy. Located on the ground floor so there are no steps to navigate, Joyce feels she is living in a house rather than an apartment building. She has made friends, found new interests and activities—bingo, ceramics, group singing—and never feels alone. Lunch and dinner are served in a cheerful, sunlit communal dining room easily accessible to Joyce with her walker. Sally and Tom visit frequently. Now that Sally is relieved of the daily burden of taking care of Joyce and now that Tom and Joyce are no longer under the same roof, they can all finally be at least friendly when they are together.

Joyce and her family certainly made what was the right decision *for them*. Given the historically poor relationship between Joyce and her daughter and the fact that they all got along better when they lived apart, living together permanently would have resulted in disaster. It is important that Joyce never asked to live with her children. Story number two has a different ending. Here, the parent wishes to live with his children and immediately makes his desire known.

When Albert, eighty-two, had to place his wife, who was suffering from advanced Alzheimer's disease, in a nursing home, he told his daughter, Sonia, that he would like to move in with her and her husband. Albert did not like living alone. His daughter Sonia not only understood his fear but knew that one day, if necessary, she would take care of her parents or parent in her home. Her mother had taken care of her grandmother, and she knew the same was expected of her.

At the time Albert moved in with his children, the latter were working, and Albert himself had a part-time job. Though hard of hearing, Albert was otherwise in excellent physical health. Sonia remarked of her father: "Everyone adored him. He was so sweet and kind. And very self-sufficient, since he had to work, do housekeeping, and cook because my mother was ill for so long."

Sonia and her husband were in their early fifties when Albert came to live with them. All but one of their children had left, and she was away at college. When she came home for vacations, Albert had to share his bath with her; otherwise the bath was his alone. Albert also had his own bedroom. A meticulous housekeeper, he kept both rooms clean and tidy. He also helped with the grocery shopping and preparing the meals. In fact, he enjoyed cooking and even maintained a recipe file.

Albert was a man of many interests. He never felt bored or demanded attention from his children. Perfectly capable of amusing himself, when he wasn't cooking or doing household chores, he read or watched TV. He wanted to be as independent as possible: he made his own lunch, took long walks, and did whatever he could to care for himself. Sonia taught him how to make rug squares, which helped fill his time particularly later when his hearing loss worsened.

Albert, Sonia, and her husband had a warm and close relationship. The standing family joke epitomized its unique nature: Sonia's husband maintained that if Sonia and he divorced, he would fight for custody of Albert. In no way did Sonia feel that Albert was a burden, and Albert was never aware that his being in his children's home restricted them in any way. Albert was certainly not a financial burden, for he had turned over his income and assets to Sonia upon moving in. Sonia did admit, however, that during the twelve years Albert lived with them they were unable to travel. The only exception was an eight-day trip to Europe when Sonia's father-in-law agreed to stay with Albert in order to keep him company. What is interesting is that Sonia said it never occurred to her that they could have taken yearly trips had they hired someone to stay with Albert. Because Albert was so easy to live with, respite was not a pressing concern.

In addition to Albert's affable personality, he neither meddled in his children's business nor complained about their going out too much. His hearing loss, which grew increasingly worse, curtailed involvement in their arguments. Sonia said of her father: "He had a marvelous personality and accepted his situation with a good deal of grace. He ate whatever was on the table, was always satisfied and never demanding." Sonia especially remembered that each morning as she walked out of her bedroom her father would greet her with a hug and a kiss.

Unfortunately, in time, Albert's severe loss of hearing affected his sweet personality. He became aloof and withdrawn, retreating to his room frequently rather than remaining with the family. He found it difficult to cope with his limited ability to communicate. Except for deafness and frailty, Albert remained in good health. He died at ninety-four in Sonia's home.

Although Sonia, with a sense of shame, told one of the authors she experienced relief when her father died, she spoke of the experience of living with him very warmly: "My father's living with us really did not interfere with our life and I would gladly do it all over again. As I look back, my only mistake was in not hiring someone to stay with him, so that my husband and I could have taken an occasional trip abroad."

For Sonia, Albert, and Sonia's husband, living together was certainly the right decision. As we explain in Chapter 5, the odds for success were all there. Sonia and her father had a close and loving relationship; her spouse also loved his father-in-law. Albert had many interests and was capable of amusing himself; he was not an emotional drain on his family. Albert was needed in his new home; he made life easier for everyone. Albert did not intrude in family business and arguments; he had respect for important generational boundaries. Theirs was in every sense a nurturing, loving family whose members were able to give one another space, respect one another's needs, and truly delight in one another's company. The elder parent–adult child bond was not only preserved but strengthened through living together.

Though Sonia's decision differed from Sally's, it was in no way morally superior. Families, like individuals, have personalities, explains the eminent psychiatrist, Dr. Alex Comfort.[1] Some are marked by warmth and closeness; others by coolness and distance. All families cannot be alike and when important decisions—like living together—must be made, the personality of the family is a vital factor. Considering Sally's relationship with her mother, Joyce, living together would have been destructive to everyone involved. In fact, relations between Sally, Tom, and Joyce improved when they lived separately, enhancing the mental health of the family structure itself. The personality of Sonia's family, on the other hand, consisted of psychological and social ingredients that made living together a positive experience.

Should Mom live with us? Each family must answer individually. Because home symbolizes the last vestige of control the elderly person has over her environment and because living together can be a great strain for all involved, every effort must be made to help Mom manage in her home. Ways exist to make Mom's home safe, manageable, and less lonely. Although for both young and old, home is where one can truly be one's self, for the elderly, the luxuries of home are the sweetest. Even if the home must be shared with a tenant or outside help, the elder remains in control of her living space. As one female octogenarian matter of factly put it: "In my little place I can do what I want! I can walk around in my slippers and bathrobe all day if I choose to. In my daughter's home, that would never be allowed."

Again, adult children must remember that most parents prefer to be independent, to do as much as they can by and for themselves for as long as possible. They prefer to have their children nearby in case of emergencies; they do not wish to live with them. Adult children must likewise remember that their parents have the inner resources and strengths to manage alone. Often, all that is needed to maintain them in their own homes is some assistance. Chapters 2 and 3 will address federal, state, and community programs that offer elders the opportunity to live in and enjoy their own "palaces" for as long as they can.

Can Mom Manage in Her Own Home?

Home Equity Conversion, Home Sharing, Accessory Apartments

Many people choose to live with their children because they are not aware of any other options, or because they do not want to accept any of these alternatives, or because they will not plan their lives until a crisis has occurred. Delaying planning until a crisis often leaves families feeling trapped and helpless, with few, if any alternatives.

In the next two chapters we will explore some of the ways that enable the elderly to remain living in their own homes.

One of the major problems for some elderly is the inability to continue to pay for the upkeep of their home. For a large majority of the older population home ownership is their largest or only asset. Over 80 percent of these older homeowners have paid-up mortgages; however, this money cannot be realized unless the person sells the home. For some of the elderly who want to remain in their homes but need added income for maintenance, medical expenses, or other financial needs, a relatively new program called Home Equity Conversion (HEC) is now available through some banks, mortgage companies, and nonprofit agencies. This plan lets the older homeowner turn part of the value of her home into cash without having to move or repay a loan. Unfortunately, it is only available in a limited number of areas, but this is changing rapidly, particularly since the federal government has recently developed an insured HEC program.

HEC plans differ according to the benefits they provide. In most plans, the cash a homeowner receives can be used for any purpose she chooses. Other plans, usually government-sponsored *special purpose loans,* mandate that the money must be used in specific ways, such as making home repairs or paying property taxes. Plans also vary according to the number of years of benefits provided; some are for a specific period of time, and others are for life. Some HEC loans provide regular monthly payments; others give the borrower an initial lump sum or allow occasional withdrawals over the life of the loan.

HEC plans also differ in another, important way. In most of them the older person borrows against the equity in the home. In other plans, the home is actually sold but the original owner is allowed to remain in the house as a life tenant. This is the *sale leaseback* option. The former are the more usual and exist in two basic forms: (1) *special purpose loans* and (2) *reverse mortgages.*

Before HEC loans became available, banks offered (and still offer) home equity loans and home equity lines of credit. These differ from HEC plans in that the homeowner must make monthly payments, otherwise the bank can foreclose and the borrower lose her house if these payments are not made. HEC loans defer payments until the end of the loan term or the death of the homeowner.[1]

Special purpose loans are the most widely used HEC plans. The first type, called the *deferred payment* loan, can be used for home repair or improvement. These loans usually charge very little or no interest, and repayment can be deferred until the death of the borrower or the sale of the house. The cash that the elderly homeowner receives to improve or repair the house can be used to make it safer, more accessible, or more energy efficient. These loans are usually offered by local government agencies but may not be available in all areas. Also, eligibility can be limited by income or assets.[2]

Karen Roth had a widowed mother who was in her mid-eighties and continued to live alone in an isolated ramshackle farmhouse. Two older brothers had died, and only Karen and a younger brother remained; he lived in a neighboring state. In recent years, Karen, who had been divorced many years before, had considered moving back to the farm. But that would have meant commuting an hour and a half each way just to get to work. Her friends dissuaded her, and she compromised by sleeping at the farmhouse one night a week and on weekends.

Her friends wondered why Karen did not persuade her mother to sell the old house and move to a city apartment near Karen. "Even if she agreed to do it, I think it'd kill her," Karen answered. "Remember, she was born in that house. It belonged to her parents. My daddy moved in when they married. She's always telling me, 'I was born in this house and I mean to die here.' But I do worry about her living alone out there. Even though I call her every day and she can reach me, what'd happen if she got sick and couldn't get to the phone?"

A suggestion by a friend in the construction business triggered an idea to convert the upstairs of the farmhouse into a separate (or *accessory*) apartment. Karen and her mother liked the idea because the apartment could be rented to a young person or couple, who might be willing to pay a lower rent in exchange for their doing some chores. "And also, it won't be so lonely out there for momma," Karen added.

The big stumbling block was money. Karen had always found it difficult to accumulate any savings, and her mother had only social security. Again, her friend in construction came to the rescue, informing her of a county coalition that offered deferred payment loans to needy home owners.

Applying for this loan in her mother's name, Karen learned that it need not be paid back until the borrower died or sold the house, at which time the loan would have to be paid by the heir or the proceeds from the sale. Since Karen knew she would inherit the house, she understood that she would be responsible for repaying the loan. She wondered whether this was the best method for financing and reviewed other HEC plans with her lawyer.

Karen and her mother rejected both reverse mortgages and sale leasebacks, since a reverse mortgage would not give them enough to finance the apartment renovation, and Karen did not have the down payment for a sale leaseback. Finally both Karen and her mother agreed that a deferred payment loan would best accomplish their aims. Though the loan would place a lien on the property, it would also result in improvement to the house and conversion of part of the space to produce income, thus increasing its value. And since the loan came from a nonprofit group charging interest below the market rate, Karen felt she could manage the payments without undue hardship when she became the owner.

"It's going to be great," she told her friends after the loan request had been granted and the construction blueprints drawn. "You know how much I love that old place. Now momma can have company out there and in five or six years when I retire, I'll move out there into a nice new apartment."

The second type of HEC loan is the special purpose loan. The *property tax deferral program* is the special purpose loan most familiar to the elderly. These are administered by state and local governing bodies, and eligibility is usually limited to low- and moderate-income people. Again, in these programs, the homeowner does not have to repay the loan until he or she dies or sells the house. This allows the homeowner to defer property taxes without becoming delinquent. In effect, the government lends older people their tax money each year that they live in their homes. Most tax deferral loans require a minimum age of sixty-five and an income below a certain level, although some states do not have any income limits. Unfortunately, this program is available in only about one-third of the states.

The third type, the reverse mortgage (RM), is the most flexible type of HEC. It works much like a standard mortgage loan, only in reverse. With an RM, the person retains ownership of the home. At the same time some of the equity is converted into money for the homeowner's use. Eligibility for an RM requires that the home is owned free and clear of any mortgage, or nearly so, and it must be appraised for a specific value. This loan is paid to the homeowner in monthly installments for life or over a specific number of years. The loan does not have to be paid back until the term of the loan has expired. At that time, the loan advances plus the interest must be repaid.

The first type of RM is called a *fixed-term* or *short-term* loan. This provides monthly loan payments of from three to no more than twelve years. When the term of the loan is over, the amount of the loan plus the interest is due. A variation on this is called a *split-term* RM, which also provides loans for a fixed period of time, but allows deferral of the repayment of the loan until the person sells the house or dies.[3]

A fixed RM is best suited for the person who needs additional income for a limited and definite period and who intends or expects to sell the house when that period is over.

A second major type of RM is called *long term* or *shared appreciation* loan. It is the only RM that provides monthly loan advances for as long as the homeowner lives in the home and defers all repayments until he or she dies, moves, or sells. In exchange for this open-ended income guarantee the borrower agrees to pay the lender an amount of money equal to some or all of the future appreciation in the home's value. In this type of loan, the factors affecting the size of the monthly advance to the homeowner are the age of the borrower, the number of borrowers (such loans can be to married or other joint borrowers), the value of the home, and the size of the appreciation share paid to the lender.[4]

The third type of RM is called a *line of credit.* This loan does not give either a lump sum up front nor a constant monthly payment, but advances a line of credit for a maximum amount. Portions of this money can be withdrawn at any time but the number and size of the withdrawals in any one year are limited. Like other RMs, the borrower's account against a line-of-credit RM does not have to be settled until the owner dies, moves, or sells the house. The line-of-credit RM is advantageous to the elderly homeowner who has enough income to take care of his usual expenses but cannot meet any unexpected situations, such as a major house repair or a costly health problem. Unfortunately, there are only a few states that currently offer this program,[5] although federal legislation discussed later in the chapter may be changing this.

The Virginia Housing Development Authority sponsors a line-of-credit RM loan. One such a loan was made to a ninety-one-year-old widow who lived in a single-family house. Her annual income was $5,146. Her home was appraised at $78,460, and the maximum equity line was determined to be $50,000. She needed these funds to pay for medical expenses, taxes, and insurance.[6]

In all the loan plans discussed above, the homeowner continues to own the home. The other major HEC plan referred to earlier is a form of sale and is called a sale leaseback. In a sale leaseback, the homeowner sells the house to a buyer, with the understanding that he or she has the right to live in that house for as long as he or she wants to or until death. In other words, the homeowner now becomes a renter with a lifetime lease. The buyer is now responsible for the maintenance, repairs, taxes, and insurance, and pays the original homeowner a down payment and monthly payments for the duration of the loan. The former owner, in turn, pays rent to the buyer. In most cases, this rent is lower than the buyer's monthly payments, so that until this loan is completely repaid the older person has a net cash income each month. The elderly seller should also receive a substantial down payment, which can be invested for additional income or used to purchase a deferred annuity. Payments from the deferred annuity can be set up to start when the monthly payments from the buyer end.

The sale leaseback has never been as popular as the RMs because most of the elderly want to continue to be homeowners and do not consider the thought of renting their own homes particularly appealing. In addition, there is the potential problem of rent increases over the loan period, which tends to make the older person uneasy. In the past few years, it has been much more difficult to find potential buyers for this program due to changes in the tax law that made it less favorable to own rental property.[7] Adult children, however, might want to consider a sale leaseback by buying their parent's home so that the latter can continue to live at home as a renter while gaining additional income.

Despite the apparent benefits of HEC loans, only about three thousand such loans were made in the 1980s. Before that time, practically none were granted because of legal obstacles since removed by federal legislation. HECs remained risky for both lenders and elderly homeowners; therefore, in 1987, Congress enacted a law creating a demonstration program that authorizes the Department of Housing and Urban Development (HUD) to insure up to 2,500 RMs to older homeowners by September 1991. The response was so overwhelming that many thousands of people had to be put on a waiting list. Fortunately, new legislation was passed at the end of 1990 that allocated funds for an additional 25,000 RMs over a five-year period.

Applications for these loans were accepted beginning in the fall of 1989. According to an HUD briefing paper, "Elderly homeowners who are 62 years of age or older and who live in a home that they own free and clear (or almost free and clear) are eligible to apply for a FHA-insured reverse mortgage from a participating lender."[8]

These insured loans allow the borrowers three basic payment options: *tenure, term,* and *line of credit.* These options are the same as those already described as long-term or shared appreciation, short-term, and line-of-credit. These insured RMs have features similar to the noninsured RMs: the older person remains the homeowner; and when the loan is due, the lender cannot collect any more money than the sale price of the house. The first and major advantage of the insured loan is that the homeowner "is protected if the lender fails to make the required payments under the mortgage."[9] There is a new feature in the 1990 legislation that enables the homeowner to set aside part of the equity in the home and not include it in the RM.

A second advantage is that in a shared appreciation loan, the monthly income to the homeowner should be higher because the reduced risk to the lender should result in a lower interest rate. A third advantage is that the borrower is not locked into a specific RM but can change to another type if any change in his or her life requires a different financial arrangement. This type of flexibility is unique to the federal program and a very important advantage to the consumer. Another positive feature of these RMs is that they will not be processed unless the older person has received counseling on the specific pros and cons. The AARP has trained several thousand volunteers and attorneys to offer this type of counseling.

The many different kinds of HEC loans provide the elderly with the extra cash they need to remain in their own homes. In addition, in most of these plans the older person continues to own the house and does not have to pay back the loan until the end of the loan period or until he or she moves or dies. The homeowner is never required to pay the lender more than the value of the house, even if the loan should exceed this amount. And as discussed, the federal government has recently developed an insurance program that removes most of the risks in these loans.

Many older people, however, may not want to mortgage their future and forfeit part or all of their children's inheritance by using some form of a home equity loan. Some may prefer to augment inadequate incomes by sharing their houses with other persons, or creating and renting accessory apartments.

It is interesting how few of the modern living arrangements for the elderly are new and how many are adaptations from the past. Anyone who lived through the Depression in a poor family will remember having to share a room with siblings in order to make room for a lodger or boarder. In those days, a space was often cleared to make room for a paying tenant who received a room and meals or kitchen privileges for his money. Often the tenants were immigrants, single persons newly arrived in this country who needed inexpensive shelter until they could afford places of their own. The lodger helped the hard-pressed family meet the rent or mortgage payment. No doubt this mutually beneficial, if somewhat inconvenient, arrangement continues among present-day immigrant populations. House sharing in areas where inexpensive housing is in short supply is the only way some people can manage.

More comfortable housing can be found, however, when homeowners are willing to share part or all of their houses or apartments with a tenant. A recent innovation in this area is the "matching agency," a public or private agency that specializes in matching homeowners with home seekers. By providing a central source of information and guidance, such agencies expedite the introduction of two segments of the elderly population with meshing needs; the homeowner for additional income, companionship, security, and possible services; the home seeker for affordable housing, security, and possible companionship. In addition, many house-matching agencies go beyond referrals and introductions to offer help in making these matches work.

The shared space allotted to a renter may come in several forms: a room or two with bath and use of kitchen and living room in an apartment or house (home sharing), or separate living quarters in a house (accessory apartment).

Zoning restrictions in some towns preclude accessory apartments, but a growing movement for change in these local laws may change this before too long. Where such conversions are permitted, other factors may prevent proliferation: (1) the desire for privacy; (2) a lack of awareness of this option by homeowners; or (3) the expense and inconvenience of conversion.

Home sharing and renting accessory apartments not only provide the homeowner with additional income but can also help alleviate loneliness. The elderly renter who does not qualify for a home equity loan can also obtain needed cash from a home sharing arrangement.

People have always rented out rooms but this is slightly different from home sharing. In the latter, the renter has a private room and bath but also shares the rest of the house with the homeowner and, unless he or she performs some services, usually pays half the cost of maintaining the home as part of the rental fee.

Martha, aged seventy, had always been completely dependent upon her husband, who had given her a life of luxury. Her only child, a son, had died in an auto accident when he was forty. His only son, Martha's grandson, lived in the southern part of the country; he telephoned and visited only rarely. Her husband's family and her friends were attentive but even that could not rid her of the depression and confusion she had suffered since her husband's death the year before. The house seemed cavernous. As she put it, "I feel like a small pebble in a huge, empty drum." When her husband's niece, who lived nearby and worked for a local family service agency, took her to see the director of the home sharing program, she was ready for a housemate. Another widow, Charlotte, had already visited the agency with her daughter and left an application.

Charlotte had very little money to spend on rent. But Martha did not need the money. She was offering two rooms (sitting room and bedroom with bath) plus the run of the living areas rent free. In addition, she would pay $100 per month in exchange for services. What Martha hoped for was an efficient house manager to cook, shop, and organize the household. And that's what she found in Charlotte.

Relieved of most household responsibilities, Martha was generous in her praise of Charlotte's competence and good nature. "I'm not very good company these days," she admitted, "but Charlotte is always patient and tries hard to cheer me."

Charlotte said that Martha was often despondent, "though not as often as when I first came to live here. It takes some longer than others to come to terms with the loss of a husband. And when she gets a really bad crying jag, I call her niece or the social worker at the home share agency."

The social worker called monthly to check on the progress of the pair and to discuss any problems. She seemed to think they were doing very well although the relationship was more like servant and mistress than one of peer companions. The binding factors in their relationship were almost entirely practical: Martha relied on Charlotte to run her household and to be a dependable presence in case of emergency; Charlotte received free room and board and an additional sum every month, all a welcome supplement to her small government pension.

Where difficult personalities are involved in a home sharing match, the role of an agency is even more critical. The case of Inez, aged 85, who came to live with Lucy, aged 68, illustrates this dilemma.

Inez had lived in an apartment with her daughter and son-in-law for twenty-two years until her daughter developed terminal cancer. When her son-in-law gave up the apartment to move in with his own daughter, Inez hoped to be taken in by one of her other four grandchildren. Distraught over their mother's illness and resentful over what they regarded as her years of sacrifice to grandmother Inez, none of them was willing to have her. They tried but were unable to find her an apartment in a senior citizen housing project. An appeal to the regional social service agency led to a referral to the county housing department's house-matching service.

Realizing that Inez was a dependent person and an unwilling participant in the arrangement, the service tried to choose a younger, more stable homeowner as a partner. This was not an easy task, as there is usually more demand from older homeowners for younger renters.

Lucy, a recently retired school teacher, had lived in her house for almost forty years, ten of them as the widow of a college professor. After her retirement she found taxes and maintenance of the house too costly and applied to the agency for a home sharer. Thus began a rocky relationship.

To begin with, Lucy complained that Inez expected to be waited on. "She wants me to do all the shopping and cooking, to serve the meals and clean up afterward, too. Then she's always asking me to drive her here and there. I didn't ask for a tenant in order to become a housemaid and a chauffeur."

Inez appealed for sympathy: "I'm old and sick. I have no strength. I still haven't gotten over this move. I'm ready to have a nervous breakdown. But you won't have to put up with me much longer. My grandchildren are coming for me soon."

With the agency's intervention, Lucy and Inez reached an agreement that they put in writing. Each would shop and cook separately: Inez would be responsible for cleaning her own room, bath, and the kitchen when she used it; Lucy would be responsible for the rest of the house; and Inez would pay Lucy a small sum for transportation.

Three years later, the two were still together, still squabbling over petty annoyances; "Lucy, your cat's on my bed again."

"Inez, I've told you a hundred times to shut your door if you don't want him there."

"Lucy, you left dirty dishes in the sink again last night."

"I was too tired to do them."

"Too drunk you mean."

And so it went. But like an old married couple, they seemed to have settled into a state of contentious equilibrium—and even to have grown fond of each other.

Would this home sharing arrangement have survived the earlier disagreements without the agency's mediation and written contract? It is difficult to say. Lucy, the homeowner, might easily have turned Inez back to the agency, creating untold hardships for Inez and her family.

The grandchildren were pleased with the arrangement, despite all Inez's earlier complaints. "Grandma's a much nicer person now," her granddaughter claimed. "Being with Lucy has made her stand up for herself, instead of depending on my parents all the time, the way she used to. She and Lucy are more like equals. And talking with the agency counselors has probably helped her a lot, too."

This granddaughter and another who lived nearby stopped in occasionally for coffee and a chat, sometimes bringing one or two of their children. At least one of them took Inez shopping once each week and made certain she was driven to all family gatherings and festivities. Lucy, who had no children of her own, enjoyed the family visits almost as much as Inez did and was sometimes invited to family gatherings as well.

In addition to peer home sharers, there are intergenerational arrangements. These usually involve both companionship and services in exchange for little or no rent. In some college towns the homesharee is often a graduate student who develops a substitute grandparent relationship with the older homeowner. Most cases of this type have turned out to be extremely rewarding experiences for both generations.

A recent study of home sharing indicates that the most important reasons given for choosing this type of living arrangement concern finances, a need for services, and a desire for companionship. The role of the agency was found to be critical to the success of these matches, since the agency can provide case-management services and can help resolve any conflicts between homeowners and home sharers. In addition, it can arrange for new matches so that the homeowner can continue to remain at home even when that requires a succession of home sharers. The study concluded that home sharing was a beneficial alternative for the elderly in need of extra income, support services, or companionship. In addition, they found that this type of arrangement reduced the strain on the caregiving family members.[10]

Renting out an accessory apartment is another type of home sharing. With this arrangement the homeowner converts part of his home, usually the upstairs, into an apartment. The rental of this unit provides added income and security without the lose of privacy. Of course, the homeowner has to obtain a construction loan (a deferred payment loan discussed earlier could be used) and must also put up with the inconvenience of the renovation.

One couple, Rose and Tony Green, created a three-room apartment in their neat red brick split level house. Vera, a widow in her early seventies, moved into the new unit and in a relatively short time was regarded as part of the family by the Greens. "Vera is like a sister to me," Rose said, describing how much she and her husband, Tony, liked Vera's company. The Greens regularly invited Vera to go shopping with them, and the two women enjoyed sharing recipes, knitting patterns, and soap-opera lore.

Tony, a large, jovial man with a booming voice, agreed. "She's friendly and nice, and we all get along just great," he said.

Like Vera, the Greens were also in their early seventies. Vera had been a widow for a long time and had no children. The couple were the first family she had had in a long time. For Rose and Tony, having a tenant meant, in Tony's words, "keeping the house that we love, our home for thirty-two years, the place where our sons grew up." With its manicured lot bordered by trimmed yews, azaleas, and neatly clipped privet hedges the house did indeed reflect their love.

Their only living child (a second son had died in early childhood) lived a few blocks away with his wife and three children. Rose and Tony were unusually doting grandparents, and the teenagers frequently stopped in, regarding the house as their second home. Rose and Tony's son, Greg, and his family had encouraged and helped with the conversion of the bedroom level into the apartment and the first level to a bedroom and bath for the couple and another bedroom for guests. Except for moving the staircase to create a separate entrance for the upstairs apartment, the living room, dining room, and the kitchen on the midlevel floor stayed the same. The house also had a partly finished basement.

"Plenty of room here. In fact, it's still too large for just two people. My Rose has a bum ticker and she shouldn't even be doing all the housework she does now," Tony said. He then proceeded to describe, with mock horror, the "mess and misery" they experienced during construction. "But I have no regrets," he hastened to assure us. "It was a good move. Not only can we keep the house, but we have extra money for luxuries, like dinner out once in a while and travel." He mentioned two visits to his ancestral home in Italy and several weekend trips to scenic areas in the country with a local senior citizen's club.

Greg was more explicit about his parents' reasons for making the change. "My dad worked as a salesman for a big food company, and he retired with a pretty good pension and his social security. That was about seven years ago. But he soon discovered that his money did not go very far, what with the price of everything, including taxes, going up. Then my mom had her heart attack, and that drained off more money. They were both really scared—about losing the house, about becoming a burden on me. So we came up with the idea about the apartment. And it's worked out real well. Now they feel secure about keeping the house, and they can also enjoy a few luxuries with the added income."

Greg found the house-matching agency. He wanted to be certain the renter would be a reputable person. "It may be a separate apartment, but it's still in the same house. And I wanted to be darn careful about who moved in," he said. He also realized that if any serious problems developed, the agency could remove and relocate the tenant, something Rose and Tony would have great difficulty doing by themselves.

For both Vera and the Greens, this proved to be a mutually agreeable and profitable arrangement. Vera had a nice apartment at a reasonable rent, plus security and companionship. Rose and Tony gained greater security in their home and some discretionary income to improve the quality of their lives. As Tony said, "The best part is that our house still looks the same outside. And inside, it still feels like our house."

Not all homeowners who convert their houses to make accessory apartments want to form close relationships with their tenants. Dorothy, the widow of a career naval officer, suffered a sudden drop in income after her husband's death. On the advice of a friend in real estate, she used her husband's life insurance money to pay for remodeling the upstairs bedrooms of her pretty saltbox cottage into a three-room apartment, keeping the five rooms on the first floor for herself and her precious collection of antiques. Dorothy found a tenant by contacting the county housing agency.

Since Dorothy valued her privacy, she was very fortunate to find Jenny, who had close family living near by. Because of this strong family relationship, Jenny did not appear to need the friendship of her landlady. This was an excellent arrangement for Dorothy, who was interested mainly in the added income from the apartment. She was in her early sixties and had many compelling interests outside the home. Her only concession to neighborliness was to knock on Jenny's door on mornings when she heard no sound of movement upstairs. Also, the two women had exchanged sets of keys and emergency phone numbers and agreed to notify each other of overnight trips. Otherwise, they led completely separate lives, a situation entirely agreeable to both of them.

Both accessory apartments and home sharing have been good solutions for some older people who want to remain in their own homes. As we indicated, through these arrangements they derive the benefits of added income and social support and security. In home sharing, the obvious disadvantages are the lack of privacy and the sharing of one's home with a stranger. However, these negatives are minimized when the need for additional income or added security and companionship becomes compelling.

These are two important choices that the frail elderly might consider before making a final decision about giving up their home to move in with adult children. The benefits of remaining in one's own home are often worth the relinquishing of privacy and other disruptions resulting from these practical and sensible programs.

Can Mom's Home Be Made Safe and Secure?

Safety and Security Programs, Repair and Maintenance Services, Special Tools and Devices

As people age and experience sensory changes and losses in functional mobility, they may find it more difficult to maneuver in their customary physical environment without mishap. It is therefore extremely important to make their homes as safe and secure as possible.

Sybil, eighty-two, widowed for more than forty years, lives alone in a small two-story town house with a large living-dining area and kitchen on the first floor and one bedroom and bath upstairs. Having lost her only child, a son, Sybil's small family now consists of a younger sister on the West Coast and a niece and nephew living nearby. She had been a factory worker and nurse's aide when she was younger but after she was married she was a homemaker.

An outgoing and attractive person, Sybil led a quiet life centered around friends and church activities. Two years earlier she had a stroke that left her weakened on her left side. Although now in a wheelchair, she can walk a few steps if aided. Her nephew converted part of the downstairs into a bedroom and small bath so she is able to manage at home. In addition, she attends an adult day care center five days a week. (Adult Day Care will be explained later in this chapter and in Chapter 9.)

In Sybil's case the rooms in her house were changed to accommodate her deteriorating health, but it is also important to make the home as safe and secure as possible. Since a major cause of death in the elderly is accidents—and 80 percent of these occur in the home—measures must be implemented to enable the elderly to negotiate their environment with few falls and other dangerous mishaps. Even an accident that does not result in death can lead to permanent disability. Homes designed for the young with growing families do not usually include safety features to accommodate the physical losses of old age.

In addition to suffering diminished vision, hearing, smell, and touch, the elderly become less stable in their gait, lose muscle strength and coordination, and may experience other losses in their functional mobility. Although these changes are usually gradual and may not become noticeable until advanced old age, for seniors who have certain illnesses, such as cardiac or arthritic problems, or serious injuries, these losses can be accelerated.

It is therefore important to assess the actual surroundings. Even small changes can make a big difference in comfort and safety. Rearranging furniture to eliminate obstacles; removing scatter rugs, loose tiles, or any other underfoot hazards and replacing them with nonskid floor coverings reduces the risk of accident. In the bathroom, installing a grab bar, handrails, and a seat in the tub or shower can prevent a serious fall, and replacing faucets and doorknobs with levers can be a great help to arthritic fingers. In the bedroom, are a lamp and a telephone close to the bed? In the kitchen, are staples and essential utensils stowed in low drawers and cupboards? Is a whistling teakettle available? Elderly persons often require simple memory-joggers to help sustain a sense of self-confidence: A large, well-marked calender, a clearly printed list of important numbers posted on the telephone, and a compartmentalized pill holder are simple, highly effective ways to provide this support.

We found that most of the people interviewed had not thought about making any changes to their homes. At a senior center, for example, where a dozen older women joined us in a discussion about safety in the home, this conclusion was borne out. A few had replaced regular shower heads with European hand-held showers, finding them much easier to use especially for washing their hair. Another person had purchased a plastic chair to place on the broad side of the tub to enable her to get in and out of the bathtub from a sitting position. One woman had handrails installed on her basement stairs; another had put railings on her deck; a third had placed hand grips on the outside stair railing so that she could grab these when the steps were slippery. They *had* given this subject some thought, but as a group they had made only relatively minor adjustments to their homes.

Ruby, a sixty-seven-year-old widow, broke both her legs when she fell stepping off a curb. Hospitalized and requiring several operations, she spent the next three months in a nursing home, recuperating and receiving physical therapy. Although she was eager to return home, she could not manage this without extensive home care services. Furthermore, she would have been confined to her room. Valuing her independence, she liked neither this arrangement nor the other alternative of remaining in the nursing home for an indefinite period.

She conferred with her son and daughter-in-law who were very sympathetic and supported her wish to return home. They asked the hospital social worker to help them figure out what needed to be done in their mother's house to enable her to live safely by herself.

Following the social worker's advice, Ruby's son and his wife made the necessary changes in Ruby's house while she was still in the nursing home. They placed railings on either side of the three entrance steps. They rounded off the bottom step and added a short rail at the back door. Inside the house, they rearranged the furniture to clear a safe and easy path through the rooms with a walker and replaced the scatter rugs with wall-to-wall carpeting. In the kitchen they only had to rearrange the cupboards so that the dishes, utensils, and food were readily accessible.

The bathroom needed the most extensive alterations. Here, they installed handrails around the tub and on either side of the toilet. They also purchased a plastic seat for the bathtub, a hand-held shower head, and a raised seat for the toilet.

Not only did these simple and relatively inexpensive changes allow Ruby to return home for her long recuperation but the doctor felt that her house was now much safer and would help minimize any potential accidents.

Some changes, however, require more costly renovations. Unfortunately, there are few programs that fund these modifications. A reverse mortgage line of credit, discussed in the previous chapter, is one possibility.

There is one program sponsored by the Area Agency on Aging in Charlottesville, Virginia, which originally received a Community Block Grant, but is now supported by local government and private foundations. This program is specifically designed to assist people over the age of sixty in assessing the changes needed in their homes in order to improve their functioning. It is targeted to those elderly with cognitive deficits and sensory impairments. An occupational therapist visits the home and assesses the difficulties the older person is experiencing and what can be done to correct these. Volunteers make the required changes and supply any appropriate safety equipment on a long-term loan basis. The area agency has also produced a video tape and a manual on how homes can be adapted to meet specific needs of older people.[1]

For improved safety in the home, we suggest the following excellent references: (1) *Safety for Older Consumers: Home Safety Checklist* by the U.S. Consumer Product Safety Commission and (2) *The Do-Able Renewable Home* by John Salmen (see appendix B).

In addition to changes in the home, there are now many tools and devices available that can make life much easier for an older person. Some appliance manufacturers have developed braille overlays for control panels on their stoves and ovens; special knob covers and knob turners for stove controls for persons with arthritis; special kitchen shelf organizers; clips for easier opening of refrigerator and freezer doors; kitchen equipment designed for one-handed operation; and plastic labels to mark appliances controls.

A motorized kitchen has been designed in Sweden and is available through an office in Saskatchewan, Canada. It has counter tops and kitchen appliances driven by electric motors.[2] An interesting bathtub-shower unit is distributed by Bathease, Inc., of Tampa, Florida. It is made of fiberglass and has a watertight door so that the older person can step into the unit without having to step over a shower sill or side of a bathtub. The barrier-free entrance is much safer than the standard tub or shower. The unit itself is designed so that grab bars can be installed easily.[3]

"Touch-on" switches make turning lights on and off easier because they require less hand movement. Available for new and old lamps, the devices are sold by Sears and other catalog and department stores.[4]

Royal Doulton, a British manufacturer of fine china, has introduced a line of cups, saucers, glasses, and flatware that require less strength and less motor coordination to use without mishap. They are so subtly designed that the differences between these new dishes, glasses, and utensils and ordinary ones are not very obvious.[5]

In addition to the need to improve home safety, there may be a need to make the home more secure. A relatively new program in New Jersey called the Senior Citizens Security Housing and Transportation Program, available free to any person who is sixty or older, provides funds for this purpose. Although this type of service may not exist in other states, federal legislation has just been introduced that, if passed, would make this a national program.

Although this security program does not have any income restrictions, priority is given to low-income and minority groups residing in high crime areas. Its purpose is to provide increased security to homeowners and renters. Administered by the area agency on aging, this agency usually allocates funds to the local police department's crime prevention unit. The home security improvements offered by this program include the replacement of doors, door and window locks and frames and the installation of door glazing, peep holes, better security for mailboxes, intercom systems, improved external lighting, and automatic timers for outside lights.[6] In addition to responding to requests for safety devices, the police also conduct housing security surveys to identify the necessary measures that would make residences more secure.

In a southern county in New Jersey the crime prevention unit in one year has helped over nine-hundred elderly people, one-third of them over the age of seventy-five. It has also given free lectures on crime prevention and has instructed older people to cut down hedges so that burglars cannot easily hide. Additionally, the police have instructed the elderly on how to identify suspicious people, how to recognize potential scams, and how to keep pocketbooks and wallets well hidden.

An example of someone who was helped by this particular program is an eighty-year-old widow who was mugged while out shopping. Because her house keys were in her stolen purse, she was forced to break a window to reenter her own home. Although she immediately telephoned the police to report the mugging, she was too frightened to leave her home or to hang up the telephone. Fearing the mugger would call to see if she were home, she sat in her house frozen in terror and isolation for five days.

Fortunately the police needed more information for their special crime unit. Failing time and again to reach her, they finally came to her front door. Once there, they were able to assess the dangers in her situation and make and implement suggestions for her safety.

The police replaced the broken pane of glass in the back window, put new locks on the front and back doors, put security pins in the first floor windows, and gave her a new sensor light. She later told one of the authors: "They were a blessing from heaven. Without their help, I would not be able to remain in my beloved little house. And I probably would have died had they not come to find me. I can't believe the whole thing—it's like a miracle!"

Other measures are available to older people that can add to their safety and security. For elderly persons living alone, particularly those at risk medically, a security alarm system can be a great comfort. These systems enable persons at home to summon help in an emergency. One such system, the Life Safety System, works at the press of a button that sounds an alarm at the local fire department. Other medical-alert systems are operated through hospitals. A home transmitter signals the hospital operator when a button on the wristband or pendant is pressed. These devices have been improved to allow voice communication with the operator as long as the person who needs help is within fifty feet of a telephone.

Another simple device is called Life Alert. It consists of a vial that can be attached to the refrigerator or the dashboard of the car. The vial contains a person's important medical information—doctor's name and telephone number, blood type, allergies, prescribed medications, special health needs, etc.—and can be very useful in a health emergency. These vials are very inexpensive, and their universal distribution would save many lives. Area agencies on aging usually buy and distribute Life Alert vials to the elderly populations they serve.

A carrier-alert program sponsored by the U.S. Postal Service monitors individuals who sign up for this service; the mailman checks each day to see if the previous day's mail has been removed from the box. In addition, volunteer organizations in many communities maintain telephone reassurance services for elderly people registered with them. (Further details are given later in the chapter.)

Safety and security are important to the older person living at home, but the house must also be kept in good repair so that it continues to be a suitable place to live. The elderly need assistance both with obtaining the appropriate workmen and in some cases with paying for these services.

Since the repair industry is dominated by small, marginal operations, an elderly homeowner often finds that he or she has been defrauded. Either the job is done poorly, or it is started and not finished, or the contractor accepts payment but never returns to do the repair. In all these cases the person has lost all of part of the cost of a repair that is not performed and/or may not have been necessary in the first place. Door-to-door solicitors are experts on preying on the fears of the elderly. A typical ploy is to use scare tactics such as telling an intended victim,

"Your foundation is collapsing and if is not repaired immediately, your house will fall down."

It may be difficult for an elderly person who finds himself in the hands of an unscrupulous repair service to get help from a family member because he or she may be unaware of the situation. An elderly parent may be reluctant to tell his children for fear that they will think he is becoming incompetent and no longer able to manage at home. Even if older people can afford the repairs, to avoid dealing with dishonest or incompetent contractors they should contact the appropriate local housing agency to obtain a list of reputable repair services in the area. Some agencies also offer follow-up services to ensure that the homeowner is not taken advantage of.

Ann, a widow in her early eighties, almost waited too long to do the necessary repairs to her house. If not for the intervention of her daughter, Marlene, the house would have deteriorated to such an extent that Ann would have been forced to move out. Marlene had not had a good relationship with her mother since childhood, because she felt that she was "nagged all the time to be tidy" and continually reminded of her failings. She had been very attached to her father, who died at an early age. This only exacerbated the bad feelings between mother and daughter. Despite this hostility between Marlene and Ann, when Marlene became aware of the bad condition of her mother's home she knew that something had to done.

Ann had lived in her neat, pretty little house for almost sixty years. From the outside, however, the walls appeared literally to be tumbling down. Boards were rotting, and the front steps sagged dangerously. Some of the storm windows had been removed; others were broken or warped and thick with grime.

Since Marlene was unable to get her mother to do anything about fixing the house she decided to enroll the help of the local family service agency. Ann refused to allow the agency worker into her house at first, but after several phone calls she reluctantly agreed to admit her. Inside, every article was clean and meticulously placed. Ann proudly proclaimed that she spent most of her waking hours dusting, washing, and polishing the downstairs rooms, where she lived. (The two upstairs bedrooms were closed off.) But the interior was sorely in need of paint and repairs: faucets dripped, ceiling and wall plaster were flaked and crumbled, linoleum needed replacing and rugs were threadbare.

Ann, herself, a tall bony woman, seemed weak and emaciated. Her steel-gray hair was pulled tightly back and coiled into a bun; her dress was neat, though spotted and mended; her shoes were worn at the toes and heels. She angrily asked whether Marlene had "foisted" the agency on her and insisted she could "manage quite well without any help, thank you."

After several visits, the agency worker was able to allay some of Ann's suspicions. By appealing to her pride in her home, she convinced the older woman to apply to a nonprofit neighborhood housing committee that offered maintenance and repair services. Services provided for the elderly, handicapped, and low-income homeowners included carpentry, plumbing, masonry, winterization, roofing repairs, and window replacement. Most of the work was done free of charge or for a small fee, with funding from various sources, such as the United Way, community development block grants, foundation grants, and neighborhood appeals.

Because of the long list of applicants, it would be at least six months before work was started on Ann's house. And so far, she had given her approval only for exterior repairs. If Marlene wished it, the caseworker would try to persuade Ann to accept interior work as well.

The caseworker also reported that the house had been registered with the neighborhood crime watch and was now on the regular patrol route. Ann also had been listed with a church reassurance service that would telephone daily as a safety check.

Best of all, the worker had established enough trust with Ann to take her shopping twice a week. The first thing they did was to buy Ann a new pair of shoes. This had been one of Marlene's major headaches. She believed that her mother feared going out alone in the crime-ridden neighborhood and consequently curtailed her shopping until she reached the point of starvation. Marlene did bring in groceries periodically, but these face-to-face encounters were so unpleasant that she did so as infrequently as possible. She was happy to pay the agency worker for her time as a shopping companion and to confine her filial duties to weekly phone calls.

"What a load off my mind!" Marlene said. "It's almost as if I'd found a long-lost sister to take over the care and coddling of mother."

On a federal level, other loans and grants exist to promote sound community development and safe and sanitary housing. The major sources of funds are Community Development Block Grants, which serve metropolitan cities and urban counties, and the Farmers Home

Administration, which serves rural areas. These programs are usually administered by state and local agencies.

The Community Development Block Grant supports a wide variety of community development, among which is neighborhood revitalization. Within these blighted areas a minimum of 60 percent of funds must be spent on low- and moderate-income people. This money is allocated to counties and cities based on a specific formula.

The Farmers Home Administration also has two major programs, sections 502 and 504. Section 502 provides loans to low- and moderate-income people for housing construction, purchases, and repairs. Section 504 assists those with very low incomes to repair or improve their homes with loans at one percent interest. These loans are considered grants if the recipient is sixty-two or older and cannot repay.

The federal departments of Energy, and Health and Human Services distribute funds to the states to be used for weatherization assistance. One such program is the New Jersey Weatherization Assistance Program, which assists low- and moderate-income people in making their homes more energy efficient. Types of services can include any heating system improvement and shell insulation, such as caulking, weather stripping, and window and door repair and replacement. These repairs are made at no charge.

The Home Energy Assistance Program (HEAP) is another federal housing program designed to help low-income persons meet home heating costs. Senior citizens (sixty or older) may apply for benefits by mail; all others must apply in person. The payments can vary depending on the size of the household, the amount of income, and the type of heating system. HEAP is usually administered by state departments of energy.

In addition to the federal programs many states and local governments offer repair services. One such example is the Residential Emergency Service to Offer Repairs for the Elderly (RESTORE). It is located in New York State and makes grants through municipal action groups to homeowners who are sixty or older and who fall within specified income guidelines. Each eligible homeowner can receive up to $5,000 for repairs.

A Lifeline Credit Program in the state of New Jersey offers utility assistance to people sixty-five or older with low incomes. The recipients receive a yearly grant of $225 towards their gas and electric bills.

In addition to major repairs and renovations, help with minor repairs and chores are also important in enabling the elderly to remain living at home. These services are usually locally sponsored. Many use volunteers, sometimes the elderly themselves who are retired carpenters and plumbers. Variously called Chore Service, Mr. Fixit, and Mr. Handyman, they enable the elderly to continue to live independently.

A county handyman service in the Northeast, for example, uses volunteers from industry, retired organizations, and churches. The workers range in age from their early twenties to well into their late seventies. "It is so hard to find someone to fix a small thing like a kitchen faucet or a lamp. I'm so grateful to the handyman service for their help," said one elderly widow.

In addition to making minor repairs, the handyman service also offers help with yard work. The volunteers, themselves reap deep rewards as a result of participating in this program. One young man said, "I get to know many older people and it makes me feel like I have lots of grandparents."

A Mr. Fixit service in the Midwest, housed in a senior center, enabled Greta, a seventy-eight-year-old divorcee, to get the help she needed. Arthritic with two knee replacements, Greta's major source of socialization was the senior center she attended for eleven years. Since Mr. Fixit was right there for her, she could arrange for what had to be done without the usual energy-draining phone calls, estimates, and other preliminaries.

Greta said, "Mr. Fixit has been a life saver for me. I don't know how I would manage my home and my life without all the things he did for me. And it was all free. I didn't have to pay for anything except a few pieces of wood." The program provided many services for her, such as repairing her appliances and some of her old furniture. In addition, the volunteer adjusted her toilet seat and installed an intermediate step on her porch stairs so that she could get up and down more easily. "But the most wonderful thing he did for me was to make me a very light high stool with a short back. He chained it to my outside railing. Now I can sit while I wait for the senior center bus. You see, I can't stand for very long, so this little stool was a godsend!" she said joyfully.

Another divorcee, Laura, in her early seventies but too frail to attend the senior center, learned of Mr. Fixit from a neighbor who was a regular attendee. She owned a house and had one son who lived in Florida. Her house was extremely dilapidated. Determined to stay in her own home, she enlisted Mr. Fixit to make some significant repairs and changes to her home.

Mr. Fixit replaced the ropes in her windows so that she once again was able to open and close them. He repaired her air conditioner and installed it in the window. He cut down her cane, which was too long for her. He put grab bars in the bathroom and repaired the steps to the basement. He installed weather stripping and caulking on the doors and windows. Even when light bulbs needed replacing Mr. Fixit was there to do the job. "And now I have someone to put in my screens in the spring and my storm windows in the fall. He also hangs my draperies in the winter and takes them down in the summer. My house looks so much nicer now and it is so much more comfortable," Laura said. Without this kind of assistance it is difficult to imagine how Laura could have continued to live in her home.

There are many other agencies and community services that can aid the elderly in their own homes. Since these will be covered in detail in Chapter 8, we will only touch on them briefly here. These programs include telephone reassurance, friendly visiting, outreach, legal services, meals-on-wheels, nutrition sites, senior centers, adult day care, transportation and escort services, home health aides, and educational and recreational opportunities.

Many surveys have been made concerning the use of community services. Unfortunately, it has been found that a significant number of older people and their families are either unaware of these services or equate them with "welfare" and refuse to consider them. Moreover, some wait for a crisis to develop before finding out what does exist. This is unfortunate, since these community resources could make the necessary difference in maintaining older people's lifestyles and improving the quality of their lives.

There are a number of different programs that offer companionship and support services. One of the best known is Friendly Visiting. A good example of this is called the Home Friends Program. It has been in existence for over two years and uses sixty volunteers. These helpers range from young mothers to working people who visit in the evenings or weekends to retirees. They do not get paid and give as much time as they can.

Madge Green, a widow, is eighty years old. She has been widowed a long time and finds living by herself very lonely. She was always passive socially and has lost all her brothers and sisters. Her two sons are very caring; one lives far away but the other one lives in the next town.

Madge is a diabetic and takes insulin. More recently she has developed arthritis. She is an avid walker and also enjoys handiwork. Her only other activity is attending church, which she does almost daily. She has very few friends, is not a joiner, and refuses to attend a nearby senior center. She also will not consider sharing her house with a "stranger." Madge needs ongoing emotional support, which obviously her sons cannot supply.

Her younger son learned of the Home Friends Program and told his mother about it. She agreed to contact them for a friendly visitor. Fortunately the agency was able to find Irene, a fifty-year-old married woman with the same ethnic background. Irene and Madge hit it off right away, and Irene has been seeing her for the past year and a half. Irene sees her at least once a week and spends a few hours with her each time. Most of the time Irene takes her out. They have lunch together at a restaurant or attend flower shows since Madge is an ardent gardener. Madge looks forward to these outings and seems less depressed and lonely.

A lesser-known service available to the elderly is in the legal area. In some communities only low-income people are eligible but others can get some initial help or at least a referral to a reputable lawyer. These legal services handle many types of civil matters, including wills, public benefits, housing, utility bills, evictions, security deposits, consumer contracts, and family problems.

A seventy-six-year-old widow named Doris has lived all her married life in the downstairs unit of a duplex house she and her husband had bought fifty years earlier. She has been widowed for fifteen years. Doris has had emotional problems, which were aggravated by the death of her husband. During the grieving period, her brother-in-law asked her to sign over her house to him, promising that he would take care of it and allow her to stay in the house rent-free for the rest of her life. Since Doris was not coping very well at that time, she agreed, but did not have anything in writing from her brother-in-law.

A few years later, her brother-in-law tried to evict her. Doris contacted a local social agency for help and they referred her to the county legal services. This agency took her brother-in-law to court. Doris won the case. The judge ruled that she must be allowed to remain in the house for the rest of her life. This was a very important ruling for Doris. With her fragile emotional state, she would have landed in an institution if she had been forced to move. She needed the stable and familiar environment of her own home in order to continue to function.

Transportation is another service that is available in some form in most areas. Many states offer reduced fares on trains and buses, and in some parts of the country older people can ride public vehicles free. Some localities have vans that are free to seniors and run on a regular route to shopping areas. Others offer a "dial-a-ride" service in which an elderly person can call a day in advance and arrange to be picked up and returned home again for doctor or hospital appointments.

Recreational opportunities are available to the elderly in senior and community centers, schools, and senior clubs. In addition, the federal government issues passes to all national parks, monuments, historic sites, and recreation areas that charge entrance fees. These passes are called Golden Age Passports and are available to anyone sixty-two or older. Most states also offer free admission for seniors to the state parks.

The most promising new trend in services to help older people remain at home is being tested in several parts of the country. It is called Life Care at Home (LCAH) and guarantees a full range of health and support services for the life of the individual. This pilot project is being funded by the Robert Wood Johnson Foundation.

A model LCAH project is being developed in northeastern Philadelphia by the Jeannes/Foulkeways Corporation. This is a joint venture between a continuing care retirement community (CCRC) and a health care system consisting of a hospital, a nursing home, and a home care agency. The Philadelphia LCAH will provide a full continuum of care under a life contract. The guaranteed services covered under this contract are acute care and physician care, one hundred days of short-term personal and skilled nursing care (patient pays 30 percent of any additional care in a semiprivate room), home health care, home health assistance/homemaker service, emergency response system, social and medical day care ($5 per day copayment), home-delivered meals ($1 per meal copayment), biannual home inspection, and many social and recreational activities. Some are included in the monthly fee; others require a modest copayment.

Other benefits not included in the monthly charge are offered on a fee-for-service basis. These include home maintenance, lawn service, snow removal, a travel club, and financial and legal planning.[7]

We have presented only a smattering of the many services for older people. The best place to find out about these services and where they exist in the community is through the area agency on aging or the state unit on aging.

All area agencies and most state agencies on aging have information and referral services. Often they have toll-free hotlines specifically for this purpose. Staff is available during regular business hours, and when unavailable an answering machine will take recorded messages. These agencies also respond promptly to written requests for information.

Although state and area agencies on aging are the focal point of information for services and programs for the elderly, other sources, such as churches, religious and ethnic organizations, family service agencies, mental health clinics, and private geriatric care managers, are also available. Senior centers, nutrition sites, health clinics, and hospitals are also clearinghouses for information on all kinds of programs for the elderly. National organizations like the American Association of Retired Persons (AARP) and the American Health Care Association can also be helpful (see especially appendix B for more information).

Geriatric Care Management, a relatively new concept, has become available in the past five or six years. Although this care is also offered by private nonprofit agencies such as family service agencies, its usual source is the private for-profit sector. In addition to information and referral, Geriatric Care Management offers a complete array of social, psychological, and health care services to families. The story of Marlene and Ann discussed earlier demonstrates the special value of this type of service.

Geriatric Care Management has proven particularly useful for children whose parents live far away. The story of Tricia and her grandmother illustrates the benefits of this service under these circumstances.

Tricia's grandmother depended on Tricia as her closest relative. However, Tricia lived one hundred miles away and when eighty-six-year-old grandmother became ill the two hundred mile round trip became extremely wearing. Tricia was forced to ask her boss for time off. She told him, "My grandmother's being released from the hospital. She's just over pneumonia and she's still pretty weak. I'd like to get her settled down at home and meet the home health aides who are going to take of her."

After Tricia returned to work, she wept and said, "Poor dear. It's taken a terrible toll on her. Her memory's been affected, and she's frail and weak. I don't think she'll ever be the same again, and she knows it. The worst part is, she's terrified of being sent to a nursing home."

Fortunately, Tricia explained, her grandmother had enough money to pay for care at home, and had given Tricia power of attorney. "What I've done is hand the whole business over to a new agency here. The people who run it call themselves 'geriatric care managers.' They'll do anything from hiring a housekeeper to packing and moving an older person to a new place. A friend of mine who is a graduate social worker started the agency with two friends who were hospital geriatric case workers."

Tricia said they had arranged for a health care agency near her grandmother's home to supply round-the-clock aides for two weeks. The agency would maintain contact and evaluate the invalid's progress during that time. Meanwhile they had listed her grandmother's fine old brick house, that is in a respectable neighborhood, with a house matching agency in the area.

"Even when Granny's well enough to manage without the health aides, she's going to need someone there at night—if not for her sake then for mine," Tricia added. "I'm not sure how she'll feel about sharing her home. But it's certainly large enough. And I think I can persuade her that she needs a companion if she wants to continue living at home."

The geriatric care manager would screen the potential home sharers and set up interviews for Tricia with those deemed suitable. She planned to introduce the person she approved of to her grandmother. Tricia also counted on the agency to engage housekeeping help and to serve as a liaison with the house matching agency, which would be monitoring the arrangement.

"If it works out the way I hope it will, it'll be a tremendous relief for me. I'll call granny often, of course, and drive up for a weekend once a month or so. And in the meantime I can try to get on with my life," Tricia finished with a sigh.

Should Mom Move to a Senior Residence?

Life Care Facilities, Congregate Housing, Government-Subsidized Projects, Group-Shared Homes

In the last two chapters we discussed how older people can make their homes more financially affordable as well as physically safer and their lives more emotionally secure. We outlined the many resources and services in the community that can help the elderly remain in their own homes. If continuing to live at home, however, is not the wisest course, other housing options for the elderly exist. Although these options are available throughout the country, some may not exist in your particular area. Since some may be too expensive and others may have long waiting lists, it is important to explore all the different housing arrangements well in advance.

Amy and Jack's experience illustrates the importance of prudent planning. They had moved to Florida and after eleven years of living in their own condominium they began to consider the future. At this point Jack was eighty-one and Amy seventy-nine. They had one child, who lived in the Midwest—where they did not want to live. As Jack put it, "I was scared. Who would take care of us if one of us became very ill or died? I was beginning to feel quite insecure living by ourselves. The high cost of nursing care has bankrupted even wealthy people. So Amy and I decided to do some reading about housing alternatives for older people and visit some of them in the area."

After exploring the subject quite thoroughly and discussing it with their daughter, they decided that a life care community or as they are now called, a continuing care retirement community, would answer their needs. This type of housing offers an independent apartment plus meals, linen service, housekeeping, medical services, (except for acute care in a hospital), and a nursing home.

They were quite fortunate to find one that they could afford that was also in their neighborhood. Amy said, "Because of this we were able to retain our ties to our cultural activities and our friends from the condo."

Jack further advised, "It is important to pick a place where the residents are compatible with you. Unfortunately, this isn't as true here. It is one of the errors that we made in choosing this place. But we like everything else about it. We like the fact that we have a contract which states that we will be cared for our entire lives, no matter what our health conditions are. We have a highly rated health center which makes me feel very secure."

Amy offered, "I love our large and attractive apartment. It's a wonderful way to live as you get older. It relieves me of my household cares like housekeeping, semiannual cleaning, and heavy food shopping. It's also a good place for people who can no longer drive since our place offers transportation to shopping malls and medical and hospital appointments."

Of all the housing alternatives for the elderly, life care communities (LCC) or continuing care retirement communities (CCRC) are usually the first choice of middle-and upper-income elderly. The contract between each resident and the CCRC guarantees health care, with the exception of hospital stays, until the end of the resident's life. For these people, the comfort of knowing that no matter what the state of their health they will be cared for is well worth the price. An entry fee paid at the time of acceptance into the facility covers all the stages of care that the resident may need in the future. CCRCs usually have nursing homes directly on their grounds. Thus, if a resident needs short- or long-term nursing care, he or she can receive the needed attention without losing touch with friends in the community. For married couples, the proximity of a nursing home can be a special blessing because it makes daily visiting easier and allows the couple to feel that they are still living together.

There is no fixed architectural style for CCRC's. They may be in a new high-rise, mid-rise, or low, garden-type building, or in a renovated older building such as a hotel or motel, school, or office complex. But in all of them, each resident has a separate, self-contained apartment, which can range from a studio with a sleeping alcove to a one- or two-bedroom apartment, equipped with one or two bathrooms, a small kitchen, and a living-dining area. Communal spaces are provided for dining, social, recreational, and hobby activities.

The monthly fee pays the rent on the unit and covers the cost of at least one meal a day, housekeeping and linen services, recreational and cultural programs, transportation, and, most important, round-the-clock medical emergency services. Unless the CCRC is a rental, a substantial entrance fee is required that is usually refundable on a pro-rated basis during the first four years. Some of the newer CCRC's also offer an 80, 90, or 100 percent refundable plan if the resident leaves or dies.

Ridgecrest Retirement Residence, a CCRC located on the edge of the town where Linda lived, was operated by a church-sponsored nonprofit corporation. There were attractive one- and two-bedroom cluster cottages and two lodge-type buildings each containing a dozen studio units. On the grounds a large, barnlike structure served as a dining room and meeting hall. The entry fee was considerable because of the expenses involved in maintaining good residential and nursing facilities. However, Linda urged her mother, Susan, who had had a severe heart attack and was currently suffering fainting spells that sent her to the hospital frequently, to apply.

"It wasn't easy getting mother to fill out the form. She insisted she never wanted to move again," Linda recalled. Her mom had moved from her large suburban house in the northwest to a nearby city apartment after her husband's—Linda's father's—death. She was several thousand miles away, and Linda often worried about her.

"I told her there was a four-year wait and no compulsion to accept an apartment if and when there was an opening. It was like insurance."

Her mother's resistance to a CCRC broke down after her best friend died. Her fainting spells became more frequent, and she seemed to lose the will to live.

By the time Linda moved her mother into a one-bedroom cottage at Ridgecrest, Susan no longer cared about where or whether she lived. As Susan looked back on that period more than a year later, she remembered, "I could accept the move intellectually, but not emotionally. I didn't make any effort to be friendly or join in any activities. If it had been up to me, I'd have stayed in the cottage all day. But management insists you come to the dining room for dinner every evening. And Linda came almost every day and dragged me out—to play bridge, to go to special luncheons and meetings. Now I belong to a regular bridge club here. And I've joined a few committees and found some good friends I really feel comfortable with."

As Susan became involved in a book-discussion group, the county art society, the residents' trip-planning committee, and volunteered for desk work at the town's birth-control clinic, her general health improved. Linda was pleased with the marked improvement in her mother's mental and physical condition and no longer worried about her living alone.

If one cannot afford a CCRC or does not want to live in a community oriented toward medical service, a *congregate residence* is another, less expensive option and does not require an entrance fee. Feld House, a fifteen-story building in the Northeast with 250 studio and one-bedroom apartments is an example of this type of residence. Started over thirty-five years ago, it is one of the oldest senior citizen housing complexes. The minimum entrance age in Feld House is sixty-two. There is no entrance fee, and the monthly fee, substantially less than in a CCRC, is for the rent of an apartment, two meals daily (lunch and dinner), housekeeping, plus a variety of social, recreational, and cultural programs.

In a busy, uptown section of the city, only a short bus ride from an urban center, Feld House is in a mixed working- and middle-class neighborhood with stores, a bank, and a luncheonette near at hand. Residents from the building who wish to be actively involved in the neighborhood can discuss politics on the park benches two blocks away or work as volunteers at a hospital or social service agency in the vicinity.

In the mornings residents prepare breakfast in their small kitchens. Residents who are disoriented or impaired have their stoves disconnected and eat in the main dining room between 8:00 and 9:30 A.M. Other residents might occasionally indulge, especially for the Sunday pancake breakfasts, at a small extra cost.

Dora is eighty-one and has lived in Feld House for five years. Getting used to the regime of eating meals every day at the same time was difficult for her. But her daughter, Shirley, supports the policy, since Dora had been careless about eating properly when she lived at home alone.

In her first year at Feld House Dora volunteered as a teacher's aide at a neighborhood elementary school. Increasing distress from her arthritic condition forced her to give up that activity. But she still involves herself in neighborhood affairs and especially enjoys arguing politics with her neighbors.

In addition, she has picked up two new interests: painting and choral singing. Both these hobbies can be pursued right in the Feld House building, for on the lower level with the crafts area and the laundry room there is a large studio with easels and work tables and an auditorium with a piano on one side and a small stage for concerts and choir practice. The Feld House community shows movies and holds parties here, too, and the full residents' council meets here as well.

Dora admits that she never had the energy for stimulating new hobbies and friendships when she had to struggle each day to keep house and prepare meals for herself. These new activities and friendships give her the impetus to get up each morning. "No matter how stiff and creaky I feel, I'm glad to get up every morning," she explained.

Like most residents at Feld House Dora awakes at the first sign of light. After a warm shower, she prepares breakfast. She is glad that this meal is not part of the service package, because she feels that old people need to set their own pace in the morning.

After breakfast she makes her bed, tidies her rooms, and heads for the elevator. Just after 8:30 A.M. the lounge downstairs is a beehive of activity. Dora is joined by two other women, and the three of them hold an earnest discussion about what they will do that day. After art class and lunch they often shop at the discount store near the bank and discuss world events as they read their newspapers.

Dora's determination and her adaptability made it fairly easy for her to make the transition to the lifestyle of congregate housing. Not everyone adjusts as smoothly. Her daughter gratefully recalls: "I've realized for a long time how wise Mom was to move to Feld while she still had the energy and health to enjoy the activities."

Shirley continues to describe Dora as a "superefficient housekeeper," who had no problems with housekeeping and shopping before she fell and broke her right hip. Dora saw Feld House when a friend moved there and right away, without discussing her decision with Shirley or her two sons, put in her application. "[Living alone] wouldn't be too easy for her now," says Shirley, "her arthritis has gotten so bad."

Although Shirley recognizes now that her mother had acted in a sensible and self-reliant way, at first she reacted very negatively to her mother moving. She felt that her childhood home was being abandoned, and that her mother was not ready for an "institution." Yet it turned out to be a good thing Dora made the decision when she did. Shirley explains that her brothers and she can now be sure that their mother is safe and eating well, seeing her doctor, and taking her medication. If her mother had tried to stick it out alone in her apartment, it would have meant a lot of work and worry for everyone.

Knowing when to make the change is critical. Dora's sister, Mary, for example, had stayed in her own apartment with her children cleaning, fetching, and caring for her. By the time she made the change to Feld House, she was eighty-eight. That was too late. She had become too despondent and infirm to take part in the activities or to form the friendships that are such an important part of the elderly's living successful and productive lives.

Although congregate housing is less costly than CCRCs, both are too expensive for those with low- or moderate-incomes and limited or no assets or savings. Elderly living on a modest fixed income would also find these two options unaffordable. However, for persons in this situation government-subsidized projects for seniors represent a practical alternative.

Avery Square Apartments, in a college town in the Midwest, proved to be the perfect solution for Edwina and her mother, Diana. In four three-story buildings built around an open court with a small park in its center, ninety-eight residents live in eighty-five apartments. With the aid of a state grant, congregate services—one meal a day, housekeeping, and personal care—can be offered to a small number of the tenants. This latter service consists of help with such things as bathing, dressing, shopping, and care of clothing.

Diana, who is eighty-three, lives at Avery Square. She came from Yorkshire, England, after her husband's death to live with her only child, Edwina, who is married to an American college professor.

"When my dad died, everything was shattered. Mum depended on him for everything. There wasn't much money. He'd been a state school teacher, and she'd earned a little giving piano lessons. And the old house was falling down 'round their ears.' Both getting on in years, you know. Then Dad's being so ill and all. It really sent Mum into an awful state of depression," Edwina recalls.

For four years Diana lived in Edwina's home without much sign of improvement in her despondency. "It really is not good for the old to live with the young," Diana comments. "I felt very strongly that I should have a place of my own. I wanted to be near Edwina and the family, of course, but I didn't want to live in their house."

Avery Square Apartments proved to be the perfect solution: only a few miles from where Edwina and her husband have lived for almost thirty years, it was ideal in terms of location, set-up, and costs. Although there was a two-year waiting list, they were patient.

A short time after Diana moved in, Edwina noticed a change in her mother. Diana began to play the piano in her living room; later she performed for the other residents in the community room and then accepted the job of accompanist at church choir rehearsals. Her social life brightened as she began to make new friends, inviting them for lunch or afternoon tea or visiting in their apartments.

Edwina is extremely gratified by her mother's transformation. "I can scarcely believe my eyes sometimes. Is this the same sad lady who moped around my house? It's really quite wonderful how her real spirit and lively nature have returned since she moved to Avery Square."

It was comforting, too, to know that although Diana did not yet require congregate services, she could apply for them if she needed them in the future. Unfortunately, government-subsidized housing with congregate services is the exception, not the rule. The majority of those living in subsidized housing for the elderly have to make do without these support services. They have to rely on younger family members or neighbors, or turn to community agencies for the needed services, or may be forced to find semidependent living arrangements.

Avery Square is only one of the original sixty-two senior projects in the federal congregate demonstration program. In addition, some states have their own such programs. In order to qualify for a federal or state subsidized housing unit, one must be sixty-two or older, fall within specified income guidelines, and be able to care for oneself. The older person pays only 30 percent of his or her income for rent. Unfortunately, in many parts of the country these housing projects have long waiting lists, and new construction has been sharply curtailed since the early 1980s.

CCRCs, congregate housing, and government-subsidized projects are usually large building complexes, with one hundred to four hundred apartments. For those elderly who prefer a smaller, more home-like atmosphere, there is an option called group-shared homes.

Edna was suddenly widowed just after her thirty-fourth wedding anniversary. But at only fifty-eight Edna adjusted relatively well to the loss. She missed her husband but she made new friends and became active in organizations dedicated to improving the local schools and protecting the environment. With her daughter, Carol, Edna attended zoning board and planning board meetings. She became president of the local chapter of the League of Women Voters and a few years later won a seat on the school district's Board of Education. Her life was full. She took courses in psychology and languages at a nearby college and played tennis and bridge regularly.

But in her early seventies, Edna developed cataracts. Despite several operations, she suffered a loss of vision that forced her to curtail many of her activities. Unable to drive, she resisted calling others to give her a lift to meetings. Instead, she began to spend more time alone in her apartment. For someone who enjoyed people and involvement, solitude was very destructive. A bout with pneumonia led to a long, slow convalescence spent partially at Carol's house. It was at this point that Edna said, "I definitely don't want to make this my permanent home. My mother lived with me for most of my married life, and she lived to be ninety-three. I won't do that to my daughter."

Although Edna knew she was not ready for a nursing home, she was fully aware that she did not have enough energy for Sun City.

When Carol mentioned the possibility of living in some sort of retirement residence or adult home, Edna snorted, "Old-age homes, you mean."

At this impasse, Carol told her mother that if she were her old self, she would not be thinking that way. With all the community projects she had tackled and the battles she had fought for others, she had no right giving up on herself. That was all the encouragement Edna needed. She was grateful that her daughter had reminded her of all her old strengths.

Once they had agreed to investigate the housing alternatives available, the two of them proceeded as though they were conducting a committee study for one of their organizations. Edna telephoned several area agencies on aging and asked for lists of senior residences and housing programs. Carol contacted the state housing finance agency and the county community development department and obtained information on new and proposed projects. Together they looked into traditional housing for the elderly as well as innovative concepts in shared and cooperative living.

After several months of exploring the different housing options, Edna decided that a group-shared home suited both her pocketbook and her lifestyle. This type of living arrangement dates back to the early eighties. In a group-shared home, at least five, but as many as fifteen, unrelated people agree to live together and share the expenses and part or even all the work involved in maintaining the household. This may sound like a sixties commune. In a way it is. In communes people lived together for the economic advantages of pooling their resources, for a sense of family, and often for security from some chaos in their lives. A group-shared home serves the same purpose: it allows older people to live more economically, provides companionship, and additionally, offers a protected place where there are others close at hand to turn to when help is needed.

The communes of the sixties were formed by private groups banding together; most group-shared homes for the elderly are sponsored by community organizations, such as churches, advocacy groups, and government agencies. Most elderly people do not have the stamina to organize such households; they would have to plan well in advance while still in command of the physical energy required to set up the complex living arrangement.

Group-shared homes operate with varying degrees of independence. In some the residents themselves do all the chores: cooking, cleaning, shopping, and light maintenance. At the other end of the scale are homes that have full-time, live-in housekeeping managers. At the midpoint are residences where paid staff or volunteers help with some meal preparations, household tasks, and social needs.

A social worker in her early forties told us more about the nature of the group-shared home and its tenants. She said, "These people aren't really a family; they have no common history to bind them together. The need for companionship, security, and housekeeping help at a reasonable cost is what brought them here." She continued, "They know they can stay for as long as their health and strength hold out. Best of all, they have as much independence as they can handle without the loneliness and insecurity of living alone or the guilt of being a burden on their children."

Valdene, where a different type of shared living is practiced, is a cluster of five three-bedroom apartments in a twenty-two-story private apartment building in a middle-class neighborhood in a northeastern city. The apartments are rented and supervised by a community service agency.

The project opened in 1979 with room for twelve residents in four apartments. The landlord gave permission to remove the walls between two adjacent apartments, thus creating a large communal space for serving the main meal each evening and for resident meetings and parties. It also housed three of the residents.

A resident manager, who lives in a separate apartment in the building, is responsible for the marketing and cooking with the help of two part-time assistants. The manager also supervises the cleaning staff and is on call twenty-four hours a day. A social worker spends fifteen hours each week with the residents, discussing problems ranging from personal feelings of insecurity and health complaints to personality clashes among apartment mates.

In the apartment shared by Lila, who is ninety-two, and two octogenarians, Jenny and Rachel, there exists the usual mix of harmony and dissension one might expect from people who do not know one another well living in close quarters. Lila, partially deaf and almost blind, has suffered a major heart attack. She has been living in the group-shared residence for five years and finds every day exciting. She attends a senior day care program; Valdene provides her transportation in the project van.

Jenny, eighty-five, has crippling arthritis that forces her to use a cane or hold on to the kitchen counter tops as she moves awkwardly around the room. Modest and proud, Jenny was upset at first at the thought of having to ask a perfect stranger to zip up her dress. "But you soon learn that living together, you don't stay strangers for very long," she explains.

The third apartment mate, Rachel, eighty-six, is a former school teacher. She had a series of small strokes after her husband's death and sometimes uses a walker when she feels shaky. She made the following assessment of Valdene: "Life here isn't bad, but it's not a bed of roses. We're all set in our ways, and we get on each other's nerves sometimes. One plays her TV too loud. One clops around the kitchen at night when she can't sleep. One leaves crumbs all over the living room."

"On the other hand," she continued, "it's good to know there's someone here to talk to and if you suddenly get sick, you feel a lot safer. And it takes the strain off your children."

Group-shared homes are for people who have some economic, physical, or emotional problems that make it difficult or impossible for them to live alone. It is this common bond that draws them together.

Of course, group-sharing participants must have a decent level of tolerance for the foibles of their apartment mates. Moreover, they must be sufficiently flexible to trade some privacy for companionship, care, and financial advantages. These homes all have the same purpose: to prolong the years of independence for the elderly person who has become too frail or impaired to continue living alone. By reducing the burdens and anxieties of adult children they help to strengthen the relationship between the two generations.

A better known housing option is an adult community. These

communities are complexes of permanent dwelling units for older adults, where the minimum age ranges from forty-eight to fifty-five. They usually require at least one occupant in each unit to be the minimum age or older and ban children under eighteen from permanent residence. (In some developments this requirement has been reversed because of new federal regulations.) Adult communities vary in size from as few as 100 units to as many as 45,000, with the average falling into the 4,000–5,000 range, and are most commonly found in Arizona, California, Florida, Texas, and New Jersey.

Often located far from town centers on tracts of undeveloped land available at low cost, large adult communities can become self-contained towns. Most have community centers, clubhouses, and a variety of sport and recreational facilities: some have their own shopping centers; a few even have some health care facilities.

Residents of an adult community need a comfortable retirement income to purchase a condominium unit and to pay the monthly fees for recreation and maintenance services and for bus or van transportation to shopping areas and medical services.

Essentially, adult communities create a carefree, secure, clean, well-ordered environment for friendly, physically active older adults who are in relatively good health—people who feel they have "paid their dues" to family and society and now want to enjoy life or play in the sun.

Another of today's retirement options is the mobile-home park. The greatest concentration of such parks is in the western and southern states, but they can be found throughout the country. Most mobile-home parks are not age specific, but some are age dense—housing large numbers of residents sixty and older. Owning or renting a mobile home is less expensive than buying a home in an adult community or paying for congregate housing or for entry into a CCRC. Many parks have clubhouses, but group activities are usually generated and organized by the residents themselves.

Some elderly, dissatisfied with living alone, choose to move into residential hotels. "Residential hotel" is a broad term used to cover a wide range of accommodations, from modest to luxurious. Those specifically designed for the elderly are called retirement hotels, some of which may have planned recreational and leisure activities. Furnished rooms, maid and linen service, and two or three meals a day are provided at costs that approximate those of congregate housing. Most hotels provide rooms and are run as private, for-profit enterprises, whereas most congregate residences provide complete apartment units and are under nonprofit church-related ownership. Residential hotel living, probably because it is less structured, is also less cohesive and less conducive to making friends and developing mutual aid and support than some of the other communal arrangements.

For the older person who is having difficulty coping with daily home chores and who needs more supervision than is given in other living arrangements, a board-and-care home may be the answer. Once a fixture in every town, in more recent times boarding homes have come to be used for the frail and for mentally and emotionally impaired patients released from institutions. They often shelter and care for adults of all ages, many of whom have not lived in their own homes for a long time. Coming from dependent environments, boarding home residents are less able to cope and require more supervision than congregate housing or group-shared living residents.

In concept, board-and-care homes are similar to group-shared homes, but the former are usually larger—twenty-five to thirty residents—as compared with the five to fifteen residents in most group homes. Smaller and less regulated than board-and-care homes, allow their group-shared residents greater control over their own lives and create a better climate for formation of a "substitute family" atmosphere.

A more recent option for the frail elderly who need personal supervision but not the care provided in a nursing home is the assisted-living/personal-care home. In this type of arrangement the older person usually has a room and private bath but may have a small studio apartment, and has all the meals in a communal dining room. The seniors' medications are carefully supervised and help is provided with dressing, bathing, and other activities of daily living.

A foster home is another possible alternative for the more dependent older person. It differs from the board-and-care home in that it is a single-family household with no more than four nonrelatives living in as paying guests. A good foster home will treat residents as family members, encouraging them to participate in normal family activities.

Board-and-care, foster homes, and assisted-living residences are li-censed and strictly regulated in most states.

Home sharing, which allows the older person to remain in his or her own home, was described in Chapter 2. This can also be an option for a senior who wants to be the home sharee.

The story of Jenny's becoming a sharee is typical. At seventy-six, she was looking for a place to live and contacted the county housing agency. Her husband, a barber, had died of a debilitating nerve disease. A gentle and patient woman, she had nursed him through the last four years of his life. Their savings were drained by medical and hospital bills. For that reason she was grateful to her only daughter and son-in-law for putting the couple up, rent free, in a three-room apartment in their two-story house. Soon after the death of Jenny's husband, however, her son-in-law had to sell the house and move his family to a distant part of the state. The couple invited Jenny to come with them but she preferred to stay in the area where she had spent most of life.

So Jenny's next move was into a room in her son's apartment in the next town. It was small and crowded. "I didn't mind that so much. I had a place for myself for most of the day. But Mike and Sulee hadn't been married very long, and I felt they needed their privacy," Jenny explained, adding that she had lived in many apartments, some large and some quite small, during her married life.

Her son and his wife agreed with Jenny and helped her find an inexpensive, one-bedroom garden apartment in town. Though not specifically designed for older people, many of the building's tenants were elderly, and they had formed a good, informal social system— looking out for and helping each other. Jenny was happy there, but after only two years the landlord decided to convert the building to condo- miniums, which forced many of the older tenants to move out.

"That was a blow. For the first time in a long time, I'd allowed myself to feel a sense of permanence," Jenny recalled sadly. "But," she added, it's all turned out for the best. Because the county housing agency found Dorothy, a homeowner, who was looking for someone to share her house. And I now have this lovely bedroom and bath and the use of a big house, and it costs me less than the rent I was paying. I'm still near my son and Sulee and the children. And I can see some of my friends at the senior center, which I can walk to every day as long as I keep my health. I'm quite content. I just hope I can live here for the rest of my life."

Clearly, the elderly have many alternatives to moving in with adult children or living in a nursing home. Continuing Care Retirement Communities, congregate housing, subsidized housing projects, adult retirement communities, board-and-care homes, residential hotels, group-shared homes, home sharing, assisted-living/personal-care homes, and foster homes are some of the options to be explored. The people described all chose or were forced to move from their homes and find alternative housing. Some first tried to live with one of their children, and some opted against this type of arrangement. In all cases both parent and adult child agreed that living separately was the best solution.

For the majority of the elderly, living with their children is not a viable solution. Wishing to live close enough to their children to enjoy regular visits and to know that should serious illness strike, a family member is close by, they prefer to live independently. After evaluating all possible choices, however, a substantial number of children and their aging parents do decide to live together.

Can Parent and Child Live Together? Measuring the Odds for Success

Guidelines to Evaluate the Suitability of Parents and Adult Children Living Together

If an elderly parent and an adult child are considering a shared household, their first step is to talk with each other about the chances for a successful partnership. Living together after so many years of separation is a risky undertaking and cannot be entered into impulsively. The more potential problems parent and child can identify beforehand, the greater the chances for a positive outcome. Personality and value clashes and other areas of conflict that signal potential trouble must be analyzed to find out what can or cannot be tolerated within the context of the shared household. With only good will at work, after open discussion, parent and child may decide that living together will activate problems long dormant and sour an otherwise friendly relationship. "Not worth it!" just may be the best decision.

Parent and child may decide to give it a try, knowing full well the road will be difficult. With eyes wide open, however, and knowledge of what might lie ahead, they will be able to navigate obstacles with a minimum of hurt and pain.

Since parent and child may be confused about the "hows" and "whats" of this kind of dialogue, we have formulated two questionnaires to help with this process. We have included questions pertaining to the quality of the relationship between parent and child and parent and spouse, as well as questions focused on individual personality traits.

Although every combination of parent and child is unique, evaluation with appropriate questions can reveal significant clues about the risks involved in a particular relationship. What appears on the surface to be unworkable may after probing and scrutiny be quite the opposite. If, for example, either parent or child cannot accept or recognize another's viewpoints or needs, that can be trouble in the shared household. Flexibility, however, the capacity to adapt to changes and differences in others, can mean success. Likewise, the greater the degree of comfort parent and child have in openly communicating a wide range of feelings to each other, the more likely they will be able to live together harmoniously.

We know of one case where a seventy-three-year-old mother, strong-willed and accustomed to having her way, found it necessary to move back in with her daughter and son-in-law following her stroke. Her personality—stubborn and unbending—seemed to make a harmonious shared household unlikely. However, the arrangement worked and did so splendidly. Both the daughter and her husband really liked and respected Mother, and neither was afraid to confront her when her tyrannical behavior became unacceptable. Mother especially loved her son-in-law, so when he told her to "stop being so bossy," she acquiesced with good humor. A close and loving relationship between Mother and Daughter and Mother and Son-in-Law and the ability of the adult children to openly communicate their annoyances offset Mother's difficult personality. All parties knew there would be problems; they also knew that they had sufficient strength as a family and as individuals to make a shared household work.

Our questionaires are hardly the final word, but they do reflect what we have learned through clinical experience and current knowledge to be the most significant areas of concern. They can indicate directions to pursue and point up issues that deserve the attention of parents and children considering living together. At the very least, they offer a framework in which to gauge the odds for success.

Although a "yes" answer to every question would be the ideal, a "yes" to most indicates a high likelihood for a satisfying shared household. The pivotal areas include whether the parent is able to see her child as an adult, thereby surrendering her authoritarian parental role; whether the

Questions for the Parent

Do you feel close to your adult child?

Are you able to share feelings and thoughts, negative and positive, on most matters with your adult child?

Are you able to respect and accept your child as an adult with needs and values different from yours?

Do you give advice to your child only when she asks for it?

Are you aware of when you are bossy?

Do you make a conscious effort not to be so?

Do you consider yourself flexible, able to adapt to changing times and values?

Can you enjoy being by yourself?

Do you have interests and activities that you enjoy and give meaning to your life?

Are you able to depend upon yourself rather than your children for entertainment and socialization?

Do you have friends or some kind of social network outside your family?

Do you genuinely like your adult child?

Do you genuinely like his or her spouse?

If you do not like his or her spouse, are you able to prevent your negative feelings from interfering in your relationship with your child and in her marriage?

Are you able to tell your adult child when you are angry with her?

Are you clear about what your goals and expectations are in sharing a household with your adult child?

Are you able to accept help from your children and others outside the family when necessary?

Are you able to forgive and forget past resentments that have occurred between you and your child in an effort to make your shared household work?

parent has a relatively full life, thereby enabling her to depend upon herself rather than her children for entertainment; whether the parent has the inner resources for emotional independence; whether the parent feels close enough to her adult child to be able to communicate her needs and feelings openly and honestly; whether the parent is flexible and capable of adapting not only to new living arrangements but to changes in cultural and social values. Although more will be said about "expectations" in Chapter 6, any set of relevant questions must illuminate expectations of both parent and child.

Parents with grown, independent children, whether they live with them or not, must learn to relate to them as peers. Parents who cannot do this because the parental role is essential to their self-esteem and identity will have an especially hard time in a shared household. With the inexorable role losses that accompany old age, it is certainly easy to understand why a parent might want to cling to this final vestige of control. Moving in with an adult child is not a recreation of an earlier environment where the parent had power. Now there is no room for such an authoritarian posture. Both parent and child are now adults, equal in status and worth.

To ask a parent to finally relinquish the role of parent as she knew it when her children were young is to ask that parent to grow—to expand her cherished, but narrowly defined, concept of parent. The power and control inherent in the earlier definition must yield to mutual understanding and respect. Statements punctuated with phrases such as "I'm your mother and, therefore, you must do as I say" or "If you really loved me, you wouldn't say that" are no longer appropriate. "I may not agree, but respect your right to say what you feel" or "I understand that your needs are important too" must dominate dialogues between parent and child. If the parent cannot *move on* while *moving in* then every pecadillo—from forgetting to turn off lights to leaving dishes in the sink—will generate anger, hostility, and emotional distance.

Parents who are willing to grow will make a real effort to discover and cultivate more meaningful ways to be parents, which will make their relationships with their adult children more intimate and gratifying. As friend or teacher or guide, for example, a parent can use all she has learned throughout her life to give her adult child fresh perspectives on the universal struggles of all human beings.

Though life today is surely more pressured and complex than at any other time and values about human beings have dramatically changed, the disappointments and frustrations that accompany making it from one day to the next are common to all eras. Elderly parents who live with their adult children and consequently see them on a more sustained basis have the unique opportunity to make a profound impact on their lives. Their wisdom, offered at critical times, may help materialistic and ambitious offspring sort out the vanities from what really matters. The elderly know that love of friends and family, kindness extended to another human being, the capacity to savor a sunset or the smell of a crisp fall morning are what make life worth living.

The elderly further know that no one is exempt from life's pain. As a result, when tragedy enters the life of a child, they frequently give the kind of solace and understanding that enable the child to survive. One daughter said of her live-in seventy-eight-year-old mother after her teenage daughter was killed in a car accident:

> My mother gave my husband and me the courage to go on with our lives. We were so lucky to have her with us at that time. She made us understand with all the right words that the loss of our daughter, though infinitely tragic, did not mean our lives were over. Mother was always there for us—to hear our cries of anger and pain. She was always there to hold us. She herself had survived so many losses that we knew she understood exactly what we were feeling. Most important, she was a living example of hope and courage.

In the less restricting role of friend or teacher, a parent might, for example, spend time chatting with grown children about the dramatic changes that have occurred in lifestyles and values. Today's elderly have witnessed the transformations of our century—from horse-drawn carriages on muddy paths to jet travel to placing a man on the moon—and are eager to share their impressions. Men and women living together without matrimony, conception of children by *in-vitro* fertilization, microwave cooking, and VCR's represent changes in values and technology sufficiently revolutionary in nature and scope to stimulate delightful and interesting discussions that become a meaningful way for generations to truly learn and understand one another.

Imagine the unique gratification felt by the parent whose grown child or grandchild *comes to her* with a problem. How much healthier than the intrusion of the parent into how much money a daughter spends on clothes or the discipline of a grandchild! All families, but especially those where parent and grown child live under the same roof are better served by respect for boundaries.

In other cultures where elders by tradition are valued for their gifts of wisdom and spirituality, living together poses fewer obstacles. As a natural rite of passage, the earlier parental role of nurturer, provider, and protector easily yields to the more exalted role of sage or teacher. Having mastered life's adversities, elderly parents possess a full reservoir of knowledge and experience. As a matter of course, children and grand-children look to them for guidance and spiritual counsel. Neither "dependent" nor the "reversed child" to be cared for, the elderly parent is esteemed for the special gifts long life has bestowed upon him or her and occupies a place of honor in the adult child's home.

Although our society is poor in the customs that promote this kind of filial relationship, valuable lessons can be learned from other cultures. Ken Dychtwald in his exciting book, *Age Wave*,[1] draws upon Eastern philosophy when he characterizes old age as a new and exciting "third age." He describes this "third age" as "the period for giving back to society the lessons, resources, and experiences accumulated and articulated over a lifetime." Dychtwald's message as it applies to shifting parental roles is clear: the developmental task for the elderly parent is to become a *third age* parent whose role or purpose is to serve as teacher to future generations. As gratifying as the earlier role, parents have yet another chance to affect their children's lives profoundly. Because their children are now mature enough to extend recognition and love, the new role may, in fact, bring richer rewards. Implicit in this new role is the acceptance by parents of grown children as peers and friends.

Parents who have many interests also do much better when living with their adult children. A widowed mother who moved back in with her daughter and son-in-law when she was sixty-eight had no problems with her new life or with her grown children. Having what gerontologists describe as a "home-centered"[2] leisure style, she enjoyed baking and cooking, creating elaborate quilts, watching television, and reading the local newspaper from start to finish every morning. She was never bored and found every day exciting and worthwhile. That her daughter worked full time and truly needed her expert domestic assistance were key to the success of their living arrangement. Although in this instance Mother's interests dovetailed with Daughter's needs, making them a perfect fit, even under less auspicious circumstances Mother would have been happily occupied.

Another seventy-three-year-old widow whose lifestyle was more "community centered" also encountered no difficulties sharing a house-hold with her adult child.[3] She had several friends, played canasta at least once a week, belonged to a senior club, and enjoyed lunching with friends. That she was still able to drive rather than depend upon her children for transportation was significant in that it heightened her sense of independence.

An eighty-five-year-old father who moved in with his daughter and her husband after his Alzheimer's stricken wife was placed in a nursing home was a combination of both types. Although his talents as a carpenter kept him busy building shelves for his granddaughters' bedrooms and fixing things around the house, he also enjoyed getting out to play bridge and attend classes in oil painting.

For both types of parents—"home centered" and "community centered"—the capacity to have interests providing high degrees of life satisfaction insured the workability of their new living arrangements. Not dependent upon their children for recreation or entertainment, they are able to create and live their own full lives within the context of their children's homes. Never a burden, they bring additional interests and diversity to the shared household. Keep in mind, however, these parents are highly functioning, both physically and mentally.

The Eriksons, in their book, *Vital Involvement in Old Age*,[4] explicitly tells us that for persons to age successfully they must accept dependence upon others. The Eriksons call this necessary and healthy dependence, "interdependence." By trusting in the kindness of others, the elderly infirm individual is able to have more control over the environment. The seventy-five-year-old man, for example, who sits home day after day because he does not want to be seen being pushed in his wheelchair has neither the freedom nor independence of the person who can accept this need for help. The latter individual through "interdependence" has enriched and enlarged his or her world. By depending on another, the interdependent elderly person can now get out, go places, and be with people. Parents with the capacity to be interdependent have come to terms with their functional losses and are generally less angry and resentful. Consequently, they are not only easier to live with but can graciously accept the help of persons outside the family, enabling their children to have some deserved respite.

Another type of dependence is unhealthy and destructive and can wreak havoc on shared households. This is emotional dependence. Emotionally dependent parents with few inner resources require constant attention in order to feel good about themselves. Self-absorbed and psychologically needy, such parents must have someone on instant call to fill their insatiable needs for attention, affirmation, and love. Even when they do not live with their children they pose serious problems. When they move in, crisis after crisis can result, and even a previously good relationship can turn sour. Ideally, they and their children do best when they live apart.

These parents, referred to as "difficult" or "succorance-seeking,"[5] did not suddenly assume their trying personas in old age. They were troublesome before they became elderly or, in fact, elderly parents. They are in essence "problem adults." Old age with its natural stresses and losses only exacerbates personality traits that they have always had. Losing a husband who had so completely cared for and catered to the "difficult" parent, for example, allows an elderly mother's demanding personality to surface again. Having no idea her parent was so emotionally needy, the adult child is shocked by and unprepared for her parent's behavior. Encumbered with other responsibilities and pressures, she is unable to substitute for the late husband. One daughter whose mother had been living with her for six months epitomized the frustration and helplessness of this situation: "I always suspected my mother was a prima donna, but I never knew just how much of one until my father died. I don't know how he put up with her. He deserved sainthood! To make her happy, I or someone would have to be with her all the time and talking only about her. When I return from work and want to be alone or want to know what kind of day my teenage son had at school, she butts right into my space with her incessant 'I this' or 'I that.' If I leave her in front of the TV because I want to go to bed early, she pouts. As far as she's concerned, I exist only to serve her."

Ever demanding, requiring constant attention, and having feelings of great entitlement, the emotionally dependent "succorance seeker" invades and transgresses whatever boundaries she can in her children's home. She insists upon being included in all her children's activities. She takes umbrage when told she cannot be part of an evening with her children's friends. Tuned only into herself, she has not the slightest sensitivity to her children's needs for solitude and privacy. If her grandchildren live at home, she not only disciplines them as if they were her own but competes with them for the attention of their parents. Like a bee going from flower to flower she goes from one family member to another demanding attention, comfort, and love. She simply cannot accept that others have lives and needs of their own, but rather expects everyone to be there for her all the time.

Such parents in combination with their distraught children can turn a once peaceful home into a raging tempest where pique is high, distance and secrecy are the norms, and the potential for emotional abuse is ever present. In one family where a father continually interrupts everyone's conversations, a son-in-law eats dinner out as much as possible. In another, where a mother follows a daughter from room to room for attention when the daughter returns from work, the daughter attends aerobic classes at work's end, hoping to return late enough to find her mother in bed. A mother without any sense of boundaries whatsoever, who straightens dresser drawers while her children and grandchildren are at work, has induced her children to install locks on their bedroom doors. Although neither parent nor child wishes this distress, the force of the demands of the "difficult" parent is of such magnitude that family upheaval is almost unavoidable. Again, living apart is the better choice when a parent cannot be content alone.

Parents who move in ought to feel comfortable telling their children whatever is on their minds and in their hearts. If a parent is not sufficiently close to her child to communicate her innermost feelings and thoughts, then she will suffer greater loneliness than when she lived by herself. Isolation and loneliness occurring within the context of a family are devastating emotions that lead ultimately to depression and physical illness.[6] Although more will be said about this subject in Chapter 8, it is important to note that if a parent does not feel safe in expressing her emotions to her child, then she will not be able to experience that vital sense of "really belonging," of being a part of her new family.

Parents who move in must have flexible personalities. They must be able to adapt not only to new physical surroundings and new family roles but to changes in cultural and social values. Accepting other, newer ways of doing things or relating to people requires openness and courage. If grandchildren live at home, parents and grandparents must be doubly able to "roll with the punches." One grandparent whose pointed objections to his thirteen-year-old granddaughter's punk hairstyle seriously strained their relationship learned that if he could not say anything positive he best not say anything at all. Opting for growth, he came to view his granddaughter's lifestyle as a window on an interesting, albeit bizarre, world. Eventually he became closer to his granddaughter and even earned the admiration of her "cool" friends. Another parent who was critical of the less stern, open manner used by her children in reprimanding their children (her grandchildren) was reminded in no uncertain terms that more is known about correct child rearing today than was in "her time" and that unless she could be supportive, she had better mind her own business!

Since opportunities for collisions are greater in the day-to-day proximity of the shared household than when parents and children live separately, measuring relevant personality and relationship factors beforehand certainly makes sense. Parents who view their children as peers, equal to them in status and worth, will not need to be bossy or "right." No-win battles for control automatically subside when parents are able to let go of earlier, no longer appropriate authoritarian roles. Parents who have their own interests and who can enjoy their own company are able to grant space to their children and respect their boundaries. Parents who can be "interdependent" and accept help from others, especially from persons outside the family, will be able to give their children necessary respite from the strains of caregiving.

The relationships between parent and child and between parent and son- or daughter-in-law are also significant factors in determining whether the generations can live harmoniously under the same roof. When parent and child have experienced the kind of closeness that fosters open expression of feelings and thoughts, then an atmosphere of trust, safety, and genuine comfort pervades the shared household. Of course, a history of love and respect between parent and son- or daughter-in-law is extremely important. (More will be said about this factor in Chapter 10.)

Even if a parent can be all of the above, the adult child must be able to do her part too. Being together again after many years apart takes effort and energy from both generations.

In fact, as we point out in Chapter 8, the adult child, the "hostess" so to speak, must bear the major share of reaching-out—not to make Mother feel like "guest" or "dependent" but to make her feel truly at home and part of the family. Before the adult child assumes herself to be equal to this essential task, she should consider the following questions.

Just as it is not possible for all parents to find their children likable or lovable, some children may not care about or feel close to their parents. Some simply do not like a parent because of a specific personality trait—selfishness, coldness, or bossiness. Others, however, neither like nor love their parent for more toxic reasons. The latter, referred to by Elaine Brody as "children without the gift of care"[7] have long histories of troubled relationships with their parents. Without love, warmth, or

Questions for the Adult Child

Are you close to your parent?

Can you express your feelings on most matters to your parent?

Do you genuinely like your parent?

Does your spouse like your parent?

If your spouse does not like your parent, are you able to deal with his negative feelings?

Can you express anger to your parent without feeling guilty?

Can you say "no" to your parent when you feel it is appropriate?

Can you still feel good about yourself when you do not receive parental approval?

Can you see your parent as a vulnerable, imperfect human being and not as a parent, all-powerful, always to be feared and pleased?

Are you flexible enough to tolerate the disruptions in lifestyle and housekeeping that result when a parent moves in?

Can you listen to your parent's expression of needs and feelings without interjecting defensive comments?

Have you ceased viewing conflicts and disagreements with your parent as an adolescent struggle for control?

Can you understand how your parent's losses affect her behavior and mood?

Can you relate to your parent as an adult and not as a child to be parented by you?

Can you see positive characteristics in your parent and capitalize upon them to improve your relationship?

Do you realize the heightened importance of taking care of yourself when you and your parent share a household?

Can you take care of your needs without feeling guilty?

Do you have activities and interests that give pleasure and meaning to your life?

Are you in tune with body changes that signal stress in your life?

nurturing and often experiencing outright abuse, these children find it almost impossible to give their parents the quality care that their parents expect of them.

Children without the gift of care or who strongly dislike a parent for whatever reason ought not to live with that parent. Plain and simple! Yet in a world where much is beyond our control, children and parents may be forced together under adverse conditions. For these children, to maximize what little there is in their relationship with their parent, outside help is a must. Support groups, though always helpful, may be less valuable in these emotionally heavy situations. Counseling with a professional therapist, however, may make a difference. It may enable the adult child to understand that her parent's abuse resulted from her parent's wounds and is not a reflection of the adult child's worth as a human being. With this perspective, the adult child will recognize that whatever she can give, considering the impoverished nurturing she received, is good enough. With this knowledge, she will experience less guilt and feel better about herself as she gives care to her parent on a most trying day-to-day basis in her home.

The adult child who cannot relate to a parent as a peer will find life in her shared household a complete disaster. Afraid to assert herself, always wanting to please her parent, she will feel like a child in adult clothing. Powerless, she will grant her parent's every wish, no matter how outrageous or hurtful to herself. Ultimately, because of her inability to speak up, she will become angry and resentful and burn out as a caregiver. Psychologically a child, unable to assess objectively her parent's needs or deal compassionately with her dependencies, she will discharge her filial responsibilities inadequately and ineffectively. Only adults who relate to their parents as equals can cope with the strain of having both generations living under the same roof.

The adult child must go beyond relating to her parent as a peer and learn to see the person behind the parent. To finally grow up adult children must see their parents as people with the same imperfections and needs as everyone else. Adult children who know the events and experiences that shaped a parent's life are already headed in this direction. Such knowledge not only helps the adult child to recognize what in her parent's personality structure is receptive to change and what is not but also frees some adult children of feeling responsible for certain behaviors. Consequently, adult children who are able to see their parents as people do not squander energy on issues that cannot be resolved.

The daughter, for example, who knows her mother has always had a negative, critical personality neither takes umbrage at her abrasiveness nor tries to change her. Relating to her parent as a peer, she informs her mother that her behavior is unacceptable in a direct and matter-of-fact manner. Likewise, another daughter all too familiar with her mother's long history of needing to be in control knows that her mother will only seek necessary medical attention when she is good and ready, not when someone else (such as the daughter) tells her to. A son who knows that his father's depression and inability to experience pleasure are the result of events in his father's early childhood does not blame himself for failing to make his father "happy."

Because of myths about old age marking a return to childhood, some adult children accept the directive to parent their parents. The misunderstanding of the concept of role reversal reinforces such folklore. Role reversal, used correctly, refers to the turning point in families when adult children become dependable caregivers to their parents. It does not mean they *parent* their parents. Yet, it is easy to understand why a daughter overwhelmed with chores such as bathing and toileting her mother might feel her parent has become a child again. Elderly parents, however, are not babies to be shaped to fit into the lives and schedules of their adult children. Issues of respect and the history of relationship patterns determine filial interactions. Consequently, although a daughter may *feel* like she has become her mother's mother, in reality she has not.

Adult children who live with their parents, and for that matter all adult children who give care, must make a special effort to be aware of any infantilization of their parents. Treating a parent as though she were a child generates anger and erodes the respect that nourishes the adult child–elder parent bond.

When adult children relate to their parents as peers, open and honest communication follows. The grown son, for instance, who views his mother as his equal, tells her without ado that he wishes to sit alone in the living room with his wife. Because the hierarchical boundary between his mother and him no longer exists, he feels free to speak with and to her as a friend. The language, sound, and spirit of such communication are loving and respectful. Neither party is hurt or rejected. The daughter who is not intimidated by her mother's parental role is able to tell her when she is angry at her for an infringement of her rights; she is also able to sound a clear "no" when it is called for.

In the shared household where the intensity of interaction between parent and child is at its highest it is easy for both parties to see each other's flaws. The positive aspects of a parent's character seem to dissolve in daily observations of disconnected chatter or obsessive ruminations about bodily functions. The burden of responsibility to reach out is on the adult child; she must make an effort to unearth and reinforce the good qualities in her parent. Tell Mom: "You know, I really admire your grit! No matter how much pain you are in from your arthritis, you manage every day to look just beautiful." Another daughter tells her live-in Mom who can be "difficult" that she genuinely appreciates the financial help that allows her teenage son to attend private school. Elderly parents need such reassurance (when it is sincere) that they still matter.

Adult children who see older persons as people with the same needs for love, pleasure, and fulfillment as younger individuals usually find living with their parents less stressful. Viewing old age as yet another developmental stage in the life cycle, they also believe their parents are capable of growth and learning. These children do not perceive the elderly in stereotypes. They don't accept the generalizations that old people are stingy, old people are self-absorbed, old people hate young people. They see old people as people, nothing more or less. With intra-household boundaries intact, they, nevertheless, want to be with their parents. They admire their ability to adapt to loss, their courage to survive, their understanding of life. Parents of such children do not feel like pariahs in their children's homes. Welcomed, wanted, and appreciated, they do not experience the isolation and loneliness common to other parents in shared households.

Adult children, on the other hand, who dread their own aging might consider taking a course in the aging process. Courses on aging are given at most adult schools throughout the country. Since loss is the central dynamic in the process of growing old, the adult child who understands its meaning will be able to respond with empathy to a parent's natural fears of abandonment and helplessness.

Rest, relaxation, and the pursuit of leisure activities are mandatory for adult children in shared households. If the parent is frail and/or disabled, the adult child must be able to get away on a regular basis to do those things that restore her identity as someone other than a caregiver. The adult child needs the reenergizing found in interests that give pleasure or laughter or are just plain fun, whatever they might be. The caregiver who sacrifices her leisure activities will inevitably be consumed by anger and resentment. Adult children in shared households should view self care as an inalienable right. They should not feel guilty, but rather realize that self neglect serves no one and the greatest gift they can give those they care for is to care for themselves. A working daughter, sixty-one years old, who takes care of her disabled mother manages to play tennis at least five times every week and never misses her Friday morning appointment at the hairdresser. Her advice to daughters is straightforward: "Try to get help that allows you to live pretty much the way you always did. The less you have to sacrifice the more patient and kinder you will be as a caregiver. And don't let little things get to you, like the disorganized state of your house. The important thing is to do all you can to stay well yourself. The bottom line is your own health."

The relationship between the caregiver's spouse and parent can also determine the success or failure of the shared household. The odds for success diminish when spouse and parent have negative feelings for each other. One wise mother told the authors: "My daughter invited me to move in with her husband and her after my hip surgery. I told her 'no way.' They fight all the time and he drinks a lot and I knew it would never work." Another daughter remarked:

> I knew we would have a hard time when my ninety-year-old dad came to live with us because my husband never liked him that much. What I find charming in my father, my husband finds obnoxious. I love my father's chatter and his stories about the past; my husband thinks he's self-centered. When my father could no longer manage in his apartment, I invited him to move in with us. He wasn't ready for a nursing home and I just didn't know what to do with him. My husband initially said it would be okay to have him with us for awhile, but that I should continue looking for appropriate housing options. Well, Dad has now been with us for eight months. I love to have him around; you see, I really like him. But my husband keeps letting me know he's had it. I'm right in the middle and stuck there. Hindsight is always perfect, isn't it? I realize now that because of my husband's strong dislike of my father, I should never have asked him to live with us. At the outset, I should have discussed with Dad the possibility of living elsewhere. The whole thing has been a disaster.

The attitude of the child's spouse toward the parent assumes critical significance when the son is the primary caregiver. In some households where the relationship between son and parent is less than optimal, the wife's good feelings for the in-law parent are what account for success. A daughter-in-law whose husband's father has lived with them for three years relates the following: "My husband and his father have never gotten along. To this day they argue like children about everything. But Dad gets along fine with me. I love him and know how to make him happy, so we are all able to make it." (More will be said about this sensitive area in Chapter 10).

Even in the best of shared households, where members love, trust, and communicate, problems are bound to exist. In measuring the odds for a harmonious shared household, however, parties are able to see with greater objectivity what those problems might be. They will know in advance what areas require work; where the strengths and weaknesses of their particular relationship lie. A parent may realize, for example, that she has difficulty being alone—including eating meals by herself—and may, therefore, need more attention than her working children can give her. Knowing beforehand this could be problem, Mother and Daughter might be able to find ways to resolve it. If they cannot and still decide to live together, they will at least know what they are up against.

Because the pull to return total care is so emotionally powerful, children invite a parent to move in from guilt. Guilt cannot be the motivator for this difficult arrangement. With strong but often distorted messages from the heart and conscience dictating what is proper filial behavior, a few informed questions bring some reason to the decision-making process.

Negotiating a Living Together Agreement

Each Generation's Duties and Responsibilities in the Child's Home

If, after considering the feasibility of Mom remaining in her own home, after exploring available housing options, and after measuring the odds for a successful shared household, parent and child decide to try living together, it then becomes necessary to identify and list the expectations, duties, and responsibilities of each generation. All parties must negotiate crucial practical matters and reach some kind of verbal agreement.

"Why an agreement?" the parent and/or child may ask. "After all, we're all adults; we love and trust one another, and if something comes up, we'll solve it. Really, the idea of negotiating an agreement among family members is repugnant. It indicates that trust is lacking in our family."

An agreement may, indeed, at first glance seem rather legalistic. It may even seem irrelevant to persons who love, trust, and respect one another, especially when those persons are all in the same family. Yet, living together is a major undertaking as complex as any human enterprise. And precisely because living together involves persons with deep emotional investments in one another—who "love" one another—a neutral structure provided by a well thought out agreement is imperative to sustain good feelings and harmony.

If the word "agreement" rings cold, then perhaps the word "understanding" is better. Whatever one wishes to call it, the point is there must be some consensus on what each generation expects of the other. Not every conflict, crisis, or contingency can be predicted, but the fewer the surprises, the better the chances for a satisfying living arrangement for everyone. Love is simply not enough to guarantee the happiness of the diverse cast of characters who play out the drama of the shared household. Said one son, whose seventy-four-year-old mother lives with him and his wife: "Talk and talk some more before your parent moves in with you until you reach a common understanding. Otherwise you cannot live together without hurt and anger. Whatever you accomplish will not be enough, but it's a necessary start."

Yet, love is the central force that brings generations together under one roof. It is also the major reason why parents and children will do whatever makes sense to create a family atmosphere that provides a reasonable amount of satisfaction for everyone. Parents want and need their adult children at this time of their lives and will accommodate them in order to be part of a living family. Likewise, adult children want peace and closeness with their parents. Both generations feel compelled to put an end to old resentments and forge new links of intimacy and friendship in whatever time is left. An agreement merits consideration as a way to protect and nourish that love through what is at best a difficult living arrangement.

Although the main purpose of an agreement is to clarify expectations and establish boundaries, its overriding aim is the preservation of respect for the differing needs and values of all family members. Its core and spirit are quintessentially human. It strives to make all involved parties feel good about who they are within a complex family unit composed of people with diverse and often opposed aspirations, interests, needs, values, and developmental priorities.

Something as banal as television rights on a Sunday afternoon, if not spelled out beforehand, can damage the relationship between a grand-child and a grandparent irreparably. Yearly vacations, left undefined in terms of who is to be included or excluded, generate feelings of deep rejection in a parent who believed that when she moved in with her children she would be part of all family plans and outings. Although sometimes these dilemmas can be settled as they arise, doing so usually strains the parent-child bond. By then, a parent's feelings may be hurt, and the children may feel too guilty to assert their needs honestly. The difficulty with resolving problems without prior guidelines is that no one really feels satisfied with the outcome or with how she behaved. Each party "leaves the negotiating table" with a sense of discomfort, feeling there must be a kinder way to settle these matters. With an agreement to refer to, where expectations have been clearly delineated, either the problem will never happen, or if it does, sensibilities and feelings will not be bruised irreparably. Both parties, having participated equally in the formation of the agreement, share equal responsibility for any infraction. Most important, with an agreement the odds are good that problems will not reoccur.

That family life is disrupted when Mom returns is only natural. The dynamics of any group is altered when new members join it. Imagine something as simple and relaxed as having lunch with an old friend. Suddenly someone uninvited but known to both parties joins the table. A relaxed duo is suddenly transformed into a stressful triangle as conversation flows less easily and the planned agenda is changed to accommodate the intruder. Even if the newcomer is welcome, the dynamics of the group alter.

When someone new joins the family constellation, the same process is put into motion. The old order is disturbed. For the family to function in a wholesome, satisfying manner again, for everyone's needs to be met, and for agendas to remain open and flexible, a new balance must be struck. Family therapists use the term "homeostasis" to describe family balance. Homeostasis, originally a term used in physics referring to the maintenance of internal stability within a system, has essentially the same meaning within the context of the family.

The challenge, therefore, to shared households is to create a new homeostasis as family members adopt new roles and learn to accommodate different realities, routines, and behaviors. With the presence of new forces in the family system, the shared household requires new rules and norms. The vehicle to establish this new balance is an agreement.

Because the generation gap at this stage of the life cycle is immense, because parents and children differ dramatically in lifestyles, experiences, and values, the risks for conflict are naturally high. Only advanced preparation will make it possible to reduce troublesome areas and avert crises. Intergenerational living is simply too loaded with potential pitfalls and human vulnerabilities to leave to happenstance. The desired goal, a satisfying way of life for everyone, can only be realized through the hard work of hammering out an agreement.

It is important to remember, as we pointed out in Chapter 5, that the capacity for growth and change is not the sole province of youth. The idea that older persons are rigid and incapable of accommodation does not take into account the resiliency of the human spirit. To deny in this way the adaptability of the elderly only reinforces the cruel and ignorant stereotype that old people like old dogs can't learn new tricks. Furthermore, as research indicates, older parents wish to be a vital part of their families and crave connection with their children and grandchildren. To effect this connection, they are usually more than willing to compromise and accommodate to necessary and appropriate arrangements.

The major areas to be discussed in any agreement when parents move into their children's homes are as follows:

1. *Finances.* Does the parent wish to contribute to household expenses, such as rent, food, household maintenance? If new furnishings, architectural changes, various safety devices are necessary, how much is each party to contribute to their cost?

2. *Social Activities.* Which family activities should include a parent and which should not? Out-of-house activities like dining out, going to the movies, visiting friends and families, and shopping excursions must be outlined and explored. In-house activities, such as dinner parties for friends, special evenings when a couple wishes to be alone, drinks before dinner, even eating meals together must be discussed and explored.

3. *In-House Togetherness.* How much physical closeness can each party tolerate? When parent or child craves solitude or privacy, how can the shared household system provide for the fulfillment of these needs?

4. *Vacation Plans.* Does the parent expect to be included in all vacations? What are the child's expectations? What will happen to the parent when the child is away?

5. *Household Duties.* If a parent is capable, does she wish to perform certain household duties? Which duties does she prefer and how does the child feel about her choices? What expectations does the adult child have for her parents in these matters?

6. *Outside Caregiving Assistance.* What are the parent's expectations regarding the use of outside help, particularly if children work? What are the child's feelings about outside help and the extent to which it may have to be used?

7. *Triangular Involvements.* What is the role of the parent when she becomes privy to marital disagreements? How ought she to

behave when she disagrees with her child about the discipline of a grandchild?

8. *Long-term Plans:* What are each party's expectations regarding future long-term care? What happens when the care a parent requires can no longer be given at home? What happens if the caregiver herself or her spouse becomes ill? What happens when children want to retire? What happens if the caregiver's children need to come home to live? How many other possible contingencies, pressures, or conflicts may require that Mom leave her child's home?

Parents who can, usually want to contribute to household expenses. Helping with mortgage payments or rent or paying their share of food costs helps them feel less dependent. At a time when parents have so little control over their lives, the sense that they are pulling their own weight makes them feel better about themselves. Many parents who have cash resulting from the sale of a home, likewise, are more than willing to pay for new furnishings or architectural additions necessitated by their moving in. The more the parent is able to contribute financially to her new household and to meeting her own needs, the less resentment the child will feel over having surrendered the privacy of her home.

Children must recognize the importance to a parent's self-esteem to be financially responsible for some aspects of her new life. Even children who do not need a parent's help must allow her this form of expression. In one household, where the family has no problem meeting its daily expenses and moving-in has given the parent a surplus of cash, that parent pays for a grandchild's private school education. In another, where a parent has a scarcity of funds, she saves what little she has to give her family a major gift. One year it was a new television set; another, a lounge chair for her son-in-law.

Whenever possible, parents usually prefer to pay for their own outside help. One mother, who requires assistance from home health aides because she had suffered a stroke told us the following: "Although I don't have much money, I feel good that I have enough to pay for my own health needs. After my stroke my daughter took off from work to help care for me. Well, she needs her job and I'm glad that I can pay for the people to relieve her so that she can return to work. There's so little I can do now. Being able to help out in this way makes me feel good about myself." Another father matter-of-factly said: "That's [outside help] what

I saved my money for, isn't it? So that I could get the help I need in my old age."

Parents and children must agree on what each can or wishes to do financially. Again, the more a parent can do to diminish her feelings of dependency, the happier she will be in her new home.

The invisible boundaries between inclusion and exclusion have the most power to hurt. Should a parent be included when her children dine out with friends? Should a parent be excluded when her children invite friends over for an evening's entertainment? Every time the family goes shopping or out to see a movie, should a parent be invited? These questions define the most problematic area of consideration when parents and children live together. When the issue is not dealt with beforehand, children and parents often feel trapped into routines and behaviors that produce emotional distance and resentment. A daughter, for example, takes her mother with her every time she goes shopping. Although she desires to be alone on some of these outings, from guilt and fear of hurting her mother's feelings, she does not assert her needs. Of course, as this pattern continues, she begins to stew inside and blame her mother for intruding on her privacy even outside of the home. The mother, on the other hand, who finds it exhausting to shop so frequently and would relish some time alone at home, says nothing for fear that her daughter would judge her ungrateful.

A professional couple who do not see each other during the day and enjoy a glass of wine together before dinner resent a father's frequent intrusions into their special time. When they finally gather sufficient courage to tell him they would appreciate this hour alone, a daughter's rage so distorts the tone of her words that her father retreats to his room in despair. Her efforts to apologize and clarify her statements are frustrated by her father's unwillingness to listen or forgive. He now retires to his room before and after dinner. Both generations are locked into a pattern they do not know how to change.

These invisible boundaries must be negotiated beforehand. Knowing that her children wish to be alone at certain times, a parent will not feel rejected when those times arrive. Knowing beforehand that her mother does not wish to shop with her every week, a daughter need not feel guilty when she sets out on her own.

People involved in intimate relationships often try to read each other's minds. Since no one can really ever know what another thinks, what happens is that people project onto others what *they* think. A daughter *thinks* her mother's feelings will be hurt; a mother *thinks* her daughter will find her ungrateful; a father *thinks* his children do not want him to be part of the family at all. Interactions based on guesswork quickly degenerate into dysfunction. This dysfunction can be especially destructive in shared households where feelings and sensibilities are more than ordinarily vulnerable.

The boundaries of inclusion and exclusion extend to and include in-house togetherness and separation. More difficult to set than boundaries for social activities, in-house togetherness refers to those times when a family member simply wishes to be left alone. No matter the reason, moments when a person simply wants to be left alone spontaneously crop up and cannot be anticipated.

Although they cannot be predicted, how they are managed can be part of an agreement between parent and child. Any party desiring time alone must feel comfortable asking for it. Parent or child must be able to say something as simple and honest as the following: "I need time alone now. It is nothing to do with you. I prefer not to talk about it, but in a little while I know I'll be fine and then we can be together again." When parents feel dependent and unneeded and children feel guilty over not being "good" children, hurts are easily come by. Agreeing ahead of time on the right of everyone to ask for these necessary moments of solitude can prevent the pain of apparent rejection.

Vacation plans can be another sore spot. If the parent is highly functional and there are children in the household, some families enjoy taking a parent along for a "family holiday." If grandchildren are close to their grandparent, vacations together can be especially meaningful. If the parent is highly functional and the grandchildren have moved out, adult children may not want to include a parent in a vacation. Since many caregiver couples are middle aged, finished with raising children and eager to spend time alone with each other, they may prefer to leave Mom at home. Whatever the decision, parents must be apprised of it before they move in. The wounds that can be caused by not discussing this sensitive area are deep and can generate strong feelings of abandonment in a parent. Knowing beforehand that she will not be a part of certain vacations, Mom will not feel rejected when vacation time arrives. In some families where a parent is healthy enough to enjoy trips and money is not a problem, children encourage and/or financially help a parent take advantage of the many vacation plans offered by AARP, Elder Hostels, and other organizations serving older adults.

Children and parents must also explore in detail what resources are available to care for a parent when children are away. Parents, of course, must play an active role in selecting surrogate caregivers. Respite care in an outside facility may be the answer if a parent is frail or disabled. Parents who only require assistance with meals or personal chores may prefer the help of neighbors or friends with whom they feel comfortable. The Meals-on-Wheels and Friendly Visitor programs fill gaps left by vacationing children. Even some personal-care communities now open their lavish facilities for respite care. Functioning parents who can and are willing to stay in one of these will enjoy their own special kind of vacation in an almost hotel-like atmosphere while their children are away. Whatever the community (and more will be said about these in Chapter 9) offers must be researched, explored, and discussed by both parent and child. If cooperative siblings are available with whom a parent feels comfortable, then a solution for respite is readily available.

Parents who are functional want to feel needed in their children's homes. Even those who are disabled desire to be useful. One mother who uses a walker manages with the help of her grandson to set the dinner table every night. Another in a wheelchair folds laundry and helps her kindergarten teacher daughter prepare arts and crafts projects for her youngsters. Winding wool into different colored balls, cutting paper into specific shapes and sizes and sorting beads, she feels that she is a great help to her daughter. Some parents serve as sitters for their grandchildren.

Some children for a variety of reasons do not let a parent help with household chores. Either Mom does not do something as well as they would like or does it so slowly that they become impatient and take over the task themselves. The temptation to grab the sponge from Mom's hands because it takes her too long to wipe down the kitchen table is powerful. We exhort adult children to be patient—do not grab the sponge! It is hard enough for a parent to feel comfortable in her child's home, let alone needed. Small tasks like wiping down a table or scraping plates into the trash can assume monumental significance for a parent who may feel irrationally beholden to her children for inviting her to move in with them. The adult child pays a small price if the job isn't done just right; the parent pays an infinitely larger one if not allowed to do it.

The issue of outside help is a delicate matter that must be settled before a parent moves in. Not only may outside help be necessary when children depart for vacations, but it is another component in the continuum of long-term care. Because a parent will be around for quite some time and because it is only realistic to assume that her good health will not be permanent, home health care options must be explored. Those parents who believe "taking care" ought to be the sole domain of their family members will find the idea of outside help especially repugnant. Many children believe as well that it is their personal duty to care for their parents. If both generations are equally committed to caregiving as a family duty, then conflict is eliminated. The more common scenario, however, is that children desire outside help, but their parents do not. Again, this area must be fully explored before parent and child share a household. Parent and child must clearly delineate when and under what circumstances outside help will be considered necessary. These circumstances may vary from the ill health of caregiver or spouse to a change in the nature of caregiving task itself or in the time pressures on the caregiver. Whatever these might be, they must be unequivocally stated in the living together agreement.

A decided disadvantage of shared households is that a parent becomes privy to family spats, disagreements and other assorted imbroglios. One mother to whom we spoke actually left her daughter's home because she could not bear to witness the more-than-infrequent fighting between her daughter and son-in-law. A father to whom we spoke disapproved his daughter's lenience with her daughter (his granddaughter). He found himself in the middle of a barrage of reprimands from both generations. The way to prevent these dysfunctional triangulations is to explain to a parent before she moves in that whenever family arguments occur, it would be best if she left the battle scene for another room in the house. Returning when peace is restored, a mother may then privately discuss what happened with her daughter. Knowing her role during these eruptions beforehand, Mother will not only be spared the pain of rejection but will know she is still valued for her counsel.

Although we place long-term plans last on our list, its importance is foremost. It is also the subject most avoided by children and parents. Up-to-date studies find that nearly half of all persons who turned sixty-five in 1990 will spend some time in a nursing home. It is mandatory that every caregiving family honestly discusses this option.[1] Avoiding the subject does not make it vanish. On the contrary, the longer parties avoid the matter, the more difficult it will be. In today's world, parents live longer but spend more of their lifespans in ill health: their children are older and have health problems of their own in addition to numerous other responsibilities. It is unrealistic to assume that children can always take care of their parents until the end.

Plans must be made for the inevitable. The time will come when it is no longer possible for a parent to continue to receive care in a child's home. A spouse may have a heart attack; the primary caregiver herself may become ill or widowed; adult children may come home to live; a couple may wish to retire to another state. The parent's health care needs may change drastically. One mother shared a household with her daughter for seven years, then had to leave for a congregate care facility because suddenly a granddaughter and her family of three needed a place to live (see Chapter 4). A father in another case had to go to a nursing home because his daughter seriously injured her back while lifting him. The point is, anything can happen to alter the status quo.

The value of an agreement where terms are spelled out is immeasurable to those especially vulnerable parents referred to in Chapter 5 as "succorance seekers." Although these parents disregard the needs of others because of their own incapacities, an agreement might be just the appropriate neutral device to warn them of what lies ahead. The very act of convening to talk about the future may leave enough of an imprint to soften the tone of negotiations when conflict occurs. The adult child can remind: "But Mom we talked about this before you moved in. Remember? So it's not something you did not know about or agree to earlier."

Of course, it is not possible to outline every crisis or contingency in an agreement. Our list is a beginning and includes the major areas to consider. As parent and child continue to discuss their decision to live together and its meaning to each, they will unearth more areas of potential tension and conflict. The more they can bring to the surface before they share a household, the more informed they will be and the less feelings and sensibilities will be bruised.

Ultimately, an "agreement" or an "understanding" is an instrument of love. Terms of agreement signify that parent and child care enough about each other to find out and understand each other's needs, hopes, and wishes—in other words, to learn who the other is.

The shared household, like a marriage or any other intimate grouping of persons, will flourish only with hard work. Parents and children living together must have the discipline and commitment required to do this work. Again, love is simply not enough! An agreement, like the assessment of the odds for a successful shared household, is one of the initial steps in the long process of living together. Although it does not guarantee that every day will be rosy, its foundation—honesty and open expression of needs and feelings—will shape future interpersonal relations between the generations.

Ensuring Safety and Privacy in the Child's Home

Ways to Provide the Best Possible Physical Arrangement for the Older Parent

In the preceeding chapter, we discussed potential areas of psychosocial conflict. The physical arrangements that ensure a safe and secure environment in the child's home are equally important. As we discussed in Chapter 4, there are many small and inexpensive changes that can be made to make a house safer for the parent. Particular attention should be paid to having a light by the bed, an unobstructed pathway from the parent's bedroom to the bathroom, no scatter rugs, and non-slip floors in the older person's bedroom and bath). The suggestions given in Chapter 4 concerning safety and security in an elderly person's own home apply to the child's home as well.[1]

In 1988, Congress passed the "Tech Act," which is designed to provide assistive devices to individuals with disabilities. Since the U.S. Bureau of Census has estimated that 40 percent of those seventy-five and over have severe functional limitations, the act should provide help to many older people. The funds are distributed to the states, and presently twenty-two states have received grants to implement this program. Although medical devices are excluded, financial assistance can be given to install adaptive doorknobs, powered wheelchairs, magnifiers, and the like.[2]

The physical arrangement of living together should ensure privacy for both generations and allow the parent to be independent and to entertain friends. At a minimum, the parent should have his or her own bedroom and preferably a private bathroom as well. In the interests of long-term harmony a grandchild should not have to give up his or her bedroom to make a shared household possible.

Marie has been living in her daughter's house for nine years. "There never was any question about Momma coming to live with us after my father died. It's taken for granted in families like ours," said Josie, a trim, well-dressed woman in her early fifties. The same cultural expectations had dictated that Josie and her husband live with his widowed mother during the first ten years of their marriage.

"Sharing the house was a big help to us financially at the beginning. But when the children came, there was constant bickering over how to raise them. Then when Denny's mother had a stroke and I had to take care of her and three small children besides, it was very rough!"

After her mother-in-law died, Josie and her husband bought their own house in the same suburban neighborhood as her parents' home. Here they had their fourth child, and for a while Josie enjoyed the status of "Queen of the castle," as she put it. When the last child started high school, Josie went to work as a secretary for a pharmaceutical firm, renewing skills she had practiced before the birth of her first child. Not long afterward, her father died.

Marie picked up the story. "After my Joe died, I sold our house and gave some of the money to Josie and Denny to buy this house. It's much bigger than their first house, and here I can have my own bedroom and bathroom—even when all the children are home," Marie said proudly, making certain it was understood that she had paid her own way.

She spoke of how she cooked and baked and helped with the cleaning. Aside from being deaf in one ear and having a slight limp from an old hip injury, Marie seemed healthy, mentally alert, and energetic. She praised Josie extravagantly, extolling her virtues as a mother, housewife, and secretary to a "very important executive." She also spoke approvingly of her other two daughters, only complaining mildly of their living too far away and of the infrequency of their visits. No, she did not ever travel by herself and only visited them when Josie and Denny made the three hundred mile trip and took her in the car.

Marie was proud of her nine grandchildren. "My Joe worked hard with his hands—a fine mason he was. But he only had a little education. Me, I went to high school, but I had to go to work before I could finish. But all my children went through high school, and my oldest girl even took some college courses. Now, I think, all my grandchildren will go to college. It's wonderful to have such opportunities, and they're wonderful children," she said, beaming.

"I know Momma's quite happy living here," Josie said later. "She's the matriarch of the household. Even though I like to cook and bake, too, I usually defer to her. And since I don't have much extra time, that's more of a help than a hindrance. The most annoying thing is that she follows me around the house all the time when I'm at home. And next is her interfering when we have problems with the kids. Lately that hasn't been so bad, partly because the kids are growing up and are away more than they are at home, and partly because Momma has some outside interests now, thank God."

Marie developed these outside interests when Josie, worried about her mother's being alone in the house all day and isolated from people her own age, tried to persuade her to go to the municipal nutrition site for lunch. Marie resisted at first, saying, "You know what the neighbors will think when they see that van picking me up? They'll think I'm going to a soup kitchen because we don't have enough food in the house."

By introducing Marie to a neighbor's resident mother who attended the center, Josie finally convinced her mother to try it—first once a week, then gradually as a daily event. Finally, Marie even joined a seniors' club that met twice each week after lunch (see Chapter 9).

"It's just great!" Josie exclaimed. "Now Momma has a few friends to talk to and play cards with. And once in a while she'll go on a day trip with the club. It's made her less intense about the family and has taken part of the pressure off Denny and me."

Although she wistfully admitted that she sometimes felt uncomfortable in her own house, Josie thought that her minor discomforts were a small price to pay for her mother's well-being. "My mother's generation grew up with the idea that it was a disgrace not to be taken in by your children after being widowed. I haven't passed that on to my kids," Josie said. "And if it should happen to me, the last thing I'd want is to live with one of them."

Josie and Marie's living arrangement has proven mutually satisfactory. Not all stories are as positive. John's sharing his daughter's home is an example of an inadequate physical arrangement that impacted negatively on John and the family. When John moved in with his married daughter, Sarah, there was not, unfortunately, a great deal of room. As a result, John displaced one of his granddaughters. This made his grandchildren very resentful.

Four years earlier when he was recovering from pneumonia he lived with his family temporarily for two months. Later it became obvious that he could no longer live alone. Sarah, her husband, and their three children lived on the first floor and basement of a two-family house. It was a railroad flat with kitchen, living room, master bedroom, two smaller bedrooms, and one bathroom. The basement level contained a bedroom and bath. Two daughters each had her own tiny room on the first floor while the son slept on the lower level.

John's move disrupted the household since one granddaughter was forced to give up her bedroom to her grandfather and move in with her sister. Furthermore, no one had any privacy since it was necessary to walk through the master bedroom in order to get to the bathroom. This also created hazards for John when he had to use the bathroom during the night.

In addition to the poor physical arrangement, John found the move difficult because he was not used to the noise, confusion, and the comings and goings of a busy household. Also, he had always eaten his dinner meal at 4 P.M.; at Sarah's dinner was served at six. This, plus being left alone all day while the children were at school and their parents at work, made John become more cantankerous and demanding.

He expected his daughter to come directly home from work (and not shop on her way home). He also wanted his daughter to be with him when she was not working. He would keep a record of the times when she was out at night. To punish her he would refuse to eat saying it was too late for him to have dinner. His loss of independence had made him unhappy and dour.

One of his granddaughters felt that he needed more social contacts during the day and found an adult day care center that provided free transportation. The socialization and noontime meal, were only minimally helpful because John had become quite frail and intransigent. The inadequate poor physical arrangements at Sarah's house, where the living space was really too small to accommodate her family and her father, played no small part in the general discomfort everyone suffered.

By contrast, Miriam, and Aaron had a very large house, and Aaron could provide his mother with her own room and bath. Mary, Miriam's mother-in-law, was a widow, aged seventy-one, when she came to live with her son's family. She was in good health but had spent her limited savings in the seven years after her husband's death, and was not able to maintain her own apartment on her modest social security. She had lived close by, and her three grandchildren visited frequently after school and on weekends. Needless to say, they had an excellent relationship.

Miriam and Aaron's house had two floors and a partially above-ground basement. The first floor had a living room, dining room, kitchen, two bedrooms, and a bath; the second floor had two bedrooms and a bath; and the lower level contained a bedroom and bath. The basement area had only been used as a play area when the children were very young or as a guest room. So when the grandmother moved in, the basement suite was ideal for her. She was removed from the noise and the clatter of the family and was able to maintain her privacy.

For the first twelve years of her residence, Mary was quite spry and was able to be a help with the household chores and the children. Since both Miriam and Aaron worked it was a real comfort to them to know that the grandmother was at home to greet the children and oversee their activities. Mary loved to wash and iron and would watch her favorite daytime television serials as she ironed. She ironed everything in sight, even rags. She also assisted Miriam with the cooking.

A few years before Mary moved in with the family, Miriam decided to return to work as a substitute teacher. After her mother-in-law lived with them she was able to become a full-time teacher and even decided to return to college and get a master's degree. Since she attended school two days a week (from 4 to 9 P.M.), Mary would cook dinner for the family on those nights.

Mary was very content. She had had very little schooling and enjoyed the simple pleasures of domestic tasks and television. She also knew enough not to interfere in the family's business. "At times she would grimace and show some displeasure when she disapproved of what was going on, but she kept quiet and never said a word," Miriam explained.

Aaron added that "mother always went to bed early and since her bedroom was on a lower floor we could entertain friends in the evening without disturbing her. And we always took her with us on family outings, which she thoroughly enjoyed."

Mary had one good friend from her old neighborhood whom she visited once a week. After a few years she joined the sisterhood of the local temple and made some new friends. She tried going to the senior center, but did not like it. However, she occasionally joined in on one of their trips.

These twelve years were good ones for Mary and the family, and it is easy to see how the excellent physical arrangements at Aaron and Miriam's contributed to the family's harmony.

Although having ones's own bedroom and bath is the preferred arrangement for a parent who lives in an adult child's home, a separate apartment, if only a studio with a kitchenette, insures the maximum privacy for each generation. This can be accomplished by remodeling the house or by building an addition.

After her husband died, Arlene had difficulty living alone and tried many different arrangements, from moving to an apartment complex to sharing a place with her brother. Since none of these worked out, she approached her two daughters and asked to move in with one of them. The older daughter's house was too small but Arlene was willing to help them move and to pay for a larger home. Her son-in-law was not too fond of this idea, particularly after she lived with them temporarily for a few months. Her younger daughter, Freda, willing to have Mother live with her and her family, agreed to build an extension to her house. The extension had its own private entrance, a kitchen, living room/bedroom, and bathroom. Arlene paid for this renovation herself, which made her feel it was really her own place and that she was not beholden to her daughter and son-in-law.

Arlene was sixty-seven when she moved into her new apartment. She cooked and ate most of her meals alone, but had dinner with the family at least once a week. With this arrangement she had both a real feeling of independence and control over her own life and the comfort of knowing that her daughter was close by. Since she did not drive, Freda took her shopping. Arlene did her part by helping in the kitchen when her daughter entertained family and friends.

She volunteered to baby-sit with her young grandchildren on occasion but not on a regular basis. In addition, she earned some extra money by baby-sitting for a few neighbors. Her daughter and a few other friends took turns car-pooling their mothers to a local senior center. Since Arlene had very few friends, the center became a very important part of her life. She met new people and even acquired a steady boy friend.

Arlene and her daughter's family had an excellent relationship. As she put it, "Having my own separate apartment made all the difference. I could entertain my senior center friends without disturbing the rest of the house. And my daughter and her family could lead their own lives without my interference. I was feeling much less lonely and anxious although I still missed my husband very much."

Marcy and Andrew, both in their mid-eighties, much older and in much poorer health than Arlene, exemplify another situation of parents who were forced to move in with their children. Andrew needed some care; Marcy was beginning to show signs of senility so that she was not able to minister to her husband's needs. Pearl, their daughter, was running back and forth trying to help her parents and often spending a week at a time at their house. Since she had a large family of her own, she felt that she could not continue to do this without completely neglecting all her other responsibilities.

Pearl had a large two-story house with a kitchen, living room, bedroom and bath downstairs and two bedrooms and a bath upstairs. Since there were still four school-age children living at home, there obviously was no room for any additional people. As her parents' condition worsened, Pearl began talking to them about moving out of their house. Her father refused, saying, "I've lived in this old place for over fifty years and I want to die in my own bed!" He did not relent until she had convinced him that she could no longer continue caring for him in his own home and that he had only two choices, moving to a nursing home or moving in with Pearl and her family.

It was necessary to build an addition to the first floor to create a living room, bedroom, and bath for the couple. This would give each family privacy and enable Pearl to care for her own family and for her parents. Pearl's husband and the grandchildren were very fond of her parents, and as Pearl's husband said, "As long as Pearl wants her parents to live with us, they'll stay."

Andrew did not want to be a burden. Since he was extremely handy, he tried to be useful by helping with some outside chores. Marcy, within her limited mental capacity, also tried to contribute to the household.

Pearl and her family are very easygoing people who enjoy an extremely good relationship with her parents. Their living together did not seem to produce any unusual strain. A separate living arrangement, granddaughters willing to stay with their grandparents to allow Pearl and her husband nights out, and neighbors who frequently dropped in to visit the elderly couple all helped make this situation comfortable.

The following story about sharing a home with an adult child has a slightly different twist. Jane is a very amiable, lively, and outgoing sixty-six-year-old woman who had lived in the same house for over sixty years. Her mother died when she was twelve, and she raised her younger brothers and ran the household. She married in 1953. Her father died soon after her marriage, and she and her husband moved into the large, rambling four-bedroom family home.

Jane has two married daughters and one grandson. When her husband died, she says that for three months "I did not care if I lived or died. I hated everyone and everything and felt like part of me had left." Basically a lively and sociable person who had entertained large groups of people for Sunday dinners, this attitude was completely out of character. She had been very active in a small senior club that meets weekly. She said, "I loved going on the trips and meeting new people. I was the court jester. I got them all laughing."

Since she was so depressed after her husband's death and found it difficult to be alone, she spent the next few months living with one of her daughters. During this time they discussed the possibility of making the arrangement permanent. Jane was somewhat reluctant since it was difficult for her to give up her home and all her friends and social life. On the other hand she and her daughter have an excellent relationship and enjoy similar pleasures. It was finally decided that Jane would live with her daughter for six months during the late fall, winter, and early spring for two years and then make a final decision.

During this trial period, they discussed what would be the best physical arrangement and how to share the household responsibilities. They decided to convert part of the house into a bedroom-sitting room and bath for Jane, the work to be paid for out of the sale of her house, so that she can have old friends visit and stay overnight. Jane explains, "My daughter and her husband can have space to have time to be by themselves. And I also like some time alone."

Jane and her daughter also agreed that Jane would pay for her share of the utility and grocery bills. Her daughter and son-in-law refused to let her contribute to the cost of the mortgage, for they feel that her paying for the renovation was more than sufficient. Since her daughter worked, they decided that Jane would prepare evening meals and do light housekeeping. After making the permanent move, Jane plans to join the local senior center to make new friends in the area.

"I'm sure it will work out just fine," Jane explains, "I'm real easygoing and so are they. I stay out of their arguments. I feel it's their problem and

I say, I didn't hear it or I was too busy when they ask me what I think when they're having an argument. I know a lot of people can't help putting their two cents in. Even with friends I don't take sides. I stay out of it." The best part is that Jane did not feel liké an "intruder" or a "guest" in her daughter's house and having the apartment made her feel almost like having her own home.

Jane and her daughter not only discussed the physical and household arrangements in advance of the permanent move, but also talked about what would happen if Jane became very frail or ill and needed more care. Jane insisted that she be placed in a nursing home under those conditions. "I took care of my father in my own home the last few years of his life," she said, "because I felt it was my duty. But now that I know what it was like, I wouldn't let my daughter take care of me!"

In addition to a separate apartment unit there is a fairly innovative way to allow elderly relatives to enjoy private but supportive housing. It is called Elderly Cottage Housing Opportunity, or ECHO housing. These are compact, freestanding, self-contained housing units that can be set up adjacent to a single family home. In Australia, where they are called "granny flats," there are more than five hundred in use. The Victoria Ministry Of Housing installs and rents the cottages, which are moved from place to place as needed.

Efficiency units can be as small as three hundred square feet, one- and two-bedroom units as large as nine hundred square feet. They are produced at a factory and can be finished in a variety of exterior designs to match the main house on the site. In most cases the cottages can be put up in one day, including electrical, water, and sewer hookups, and can be disassembled in the same amount of time.

The drawback is that zoning codes and public attitudes have severely limited the use of ECHO housing in this country. Although the idea has been floating around for many years attracting wide attention and a few localities have passed permissive legislation, very few units have been installed so far.

A rural county in one eastern state has started a demonstration program with three elder cottages. Each cottage contains a bedroom, living room, dining area, kitchen, and bath. Purchase price and installation costs total about $20,000. The county retains ownership of the cottages, and tenants pay a monthly rental fee that can be as low as $250. The rent is used to cover the cost of installation, insurance, and maintenance and to build a fund for the purchase of additional units in the future. When the cottage is no longer needed in one location, the county will move it to another.

Most applicants, according to the program director, were widows in their seventies, frail but still able to manage, who wanted or needed to move closer to their children. The children signaled their consent by registering as joint applicants.

Margaret, a seventy-six-year-old widow with limited income and arthritic legs, is a typical candidate. For several years after her husband died, she rented the upstairs apartment in a two-family house. But the stairs became too difficult for her, and she had to leave, giving away or selling some of her furniture. After that, Margaret lived with her son's family in a small house in town for three months, then moved to her daughter's house outside of town for the next three months, before moving back with her son for another three months. She had signed up for an apartment in a senior housing project, but there was a waiting list of several years; in addition, the project was more than thirty miles from her hometown and her family.

"The cottage has been a godsend," said Margaret's daughter, Bridget. "Ma's close enough so that we can keep an eye on her. Yet she can putter around all on her own without getting underfoot in my house, which isn't very large, as you can see." Bridget and her husband were the coapplicants for the cottage because their house stood on a one-acre lot, whereas her brother in town had no room for the cottage next to his house.

"My mother is a simple woman," Bridget said. "She's never done any other job than being a housewife and mother. She never even learned to drive. She's always depended on someone else for transportation—first my dad, now me and my brother. Anyway, I can't tell you how much it means to have her nearby, safe and sound in my backyard."

The cottage, about twenty feet behind the house, cannot be seen from the front yard. A miniature house complete with white plastic siding and black asphalt roof, it resembles the main house but is much newer and brighter.

Margaret welcomed us inside cheerfully. The aroma of cinnamon and ginger filled the neat little house, so that it was no surprise when our hostess, a woman of median height, large girth, and hobbling movements, told us she had just baked some cookies and offered us a cup of tea.

The interior is much like a motel unit, with imitation wood paneling on the walls, sturdy carpeting on the floors, and ceilings made of pressed plastic. But Margaret's furnishings overcame the sterility of the basic decor. Handmade quilts, afghans, pillows, scarves, and doilies adorned the furniture, which was old but polished and clean. The small kitchen and the bath had bright new appliances, easy to use and clean, and such safety features as a grab bar on the wall next to the commode and a plastic seat in the molded shower. The doorways are wide enough to accommodate a wheelchair, should it be needed.

Margaret exuded pride and contentment. "I haven't ever had such new things, not anywhere I've lived. It's a dear little house, and I love taking care of it. And think how nice it is to have Bridget and Bob next door, and the children to drop in on their old granny when they're at home."

In another corner of the same county, an eighty-one-year-old widow, Frieda, had just moved into an elder cottage next to her grandson's house. The old house and the three acres around it had been part of the truck farm she and her husband had owned and worked during the thirty years of their marriage. After her husband's death, Frieda held onto the farm for twenty more years, trying to eke out a living with the help of her two sons, gradually selling off parcels of land until only the house and the three acres remained.

"Neither of my boys wanted the house. They'd had their fill of farming. The younger one went to Texas to work for an oil company. My oldest rents a place in town and works down near the city in some sort of defense plant. It's his son who owns the old house," Frieda explained, pointing out the window.

She went on to tell how her grandson, Paul, had offered to buy the house after his marriage about ten years before but insisted that she continue to live there. "He's a good boy. Works in the same plant his poppa does. And he tries to keep the house in good shape, too, and puts in a big vegetable garden every spring. It makes me happy to see it."

Frieda said she had stayed in the house for almost five years until her grandson's third baby was born. "Oh I love my darling greatgrand-children, but the house was getting so crowded and noisy. And I knew they needed my room for the new baby. So it was time to leave."

With the help of her family, Frieda found a second-floor apartment in an old house in town. The only access to the apartment, however, was a long flight of metal stairs outside the house. "At first I could climb the steps with only a little huffing and puffing. But as time went on it got harder and harder. Then I stopped going out altogether unless one of the children came to help me. But I stuck it out for a few years. And I'd still be there if not for this little cottage."

A tall, once sturdy woman now withered and bent, Frieda leaned heavily on her cane when she walked. But her firm voice and rugged face conveyed strength and determination. "I may be old and worn, but I'm not yet ready for a nursing home. I never will be. I'd have stayed in that apartment come hell or high water. But it would have been lonely," she admitted.

"Here I can work in the yard, stop and talk to the children, look after the little ones. Often they are over here. Once a week I cook something special for the family, and we take it over to the big house and have dinner together. It's good to be sharing this place with the new generations." Frieda paused, then continued with passion, "We old folks should pass on our property to our children, but we shouldn't let ourselves be pushed out of the picture while we're still around. This is my home, too. I belong here."

Because of emotional ties and generational differences, a shared household often leads to irritations and conflicts. As we have indicated, a separate apartment can improve the situation. An elder cottage on the same property increases the distance between the two dwellings, allowing even more privacy for each generation, which minimizes the opportunity for conflict between parent and child.

How to Keep the Harmony

Strategies Outlining the Best Possible Psychosocial Arrangement

"Happy families are all alike; every unhappy family is unhappy in its own way." This is the famous first sentence to Tolstoy's *Anna Karenina*. Happy families are indeed alike! Happy families emanate closeness, love, and a feeling of safety; members of a happy family can say whatever is on their minds and in their hearts. In happy families, members feel good about themselves because no one is made to feel ashamed or inadequate about feelings, thoughts, or behaviors.

Tolstoy—one of literature's greatest psychologists—did not realize, however, that although every unhappy family may be unhappy in its own way, all unhappy families do have in common an inability to communicate honestly and openly to one another their innermost emotions. In unhappy families, the freedom to express hurt, anger, disappointment, frustration, and resentment does not exist. Unhappy families today are called "dysfunctional." In dysfunctional families, members are stuck in rigid, closed systems; openness is discouraged, if not feared; and blame, control, and manipulation prevent growth and change.

Continuous effort is required to produce families where members can feel safe expressing their feelings and where they can feel good about who they are. Two- and three-generation families composed of adults, however, require more work and insight on the part of members. Each generation is at a different level of development with different needs. The personalities of individual family members have been shaped by their own particular life histories. Accommodation, acceptance, and respect for the present life position and needs of family members is much harder. When parents and children have been physically separated for many years and each has formed new ways of living and thinking, even greater effort is required to keep the harmony within the family.

The simple, yet astounding, fact is that when parents and young children live together, everyone seems to know what is expected and how to behave. Parents feel and know they are there to provide their children with protection, emotional support, guidance, and discipline.

When elderly parents, however, move in with their adult children, the old rules no longer apply. The balance of power has shifted significantly. Both parents and grown children feel confused; generational boundaries, once so fixed and clearly understood, now seem fluid and inexplicable. Power once appropriately held by the parents must now be realigned. Each generation feels uncertain and insecure in its new relationship. Parents wonder about the nature of their role on their children's turf. Children, hoping to sustain respect for and peace with their parents, likewise worry over what is expected of them at a time when they no longer need their parents as they once did.

Parent and child, together again after so many, many years! How do they talk to each other? How do they behave with each other? What is right and proper filial etiquette when parent and grown child become "house-sharers" at this time of their lives? What are the new rules? What are the crucial factors that generate closeness, openess, and harmony in intergenerational living?

Families whose members are emotionally blocked and unable to express their needs are families that are troubled. The often tragic consequences resulting from lack of meaningful emotional communication in a family are the stuff of great novels, but most of us would prefer to avoid such anxiety and stress in our daily lives. Good communication skills—talking *and* listening—can be learned.[1] Once mastered, they will enhance family harmony.

The late Virginia Satir, a pioneer in family therapy, saw "communication as a huge umbrella that covers and affects all that goes on between human beings."[2] Certainly, in multigenerational families under the same roof whose patterns of parent-child communication were learned in a different context at a different time, trouble can and will result if new ways of listening and talking are not learned. Parents and children rejoined in this way often fall into old communications habits that are not only irrelevant to their new living situation but create distance and misunderstanding. Furthermore, and of greater importance, if emotionally dishonest communication styles are allowed to continue, they can actually play a significant part in undermining the physical health of both the elderly parent and the adult child.[3]

The story of Charlotte, a seventy-six-year-old widow who had lived with her daughter, Wendy, for a year illustrates the effects of poor communication on the health of the parent. Because she could not tell her daughter she felt she was a burden and unneeded, Charlotte would retreat to her room early in the evening, leaving her dinner virtually untouched. In fact, she became so quiet and withdrawn that Wendy described her as "the invisible old lady." At her wit's end over her mother's change in mood and excessive weight loss, Wendy persuaded Charlotte to see their family physician. Diagnosing her condition as depression, with gentle probing the doctor was able to discover what was troubling Charlotte and inform Wendy. As soon as Charlotte was able to communicate to Wendy what was upsetting her, she regained her appetite and became not only a "visible" but an active member of the family.

Had Charlotte from the start felt comfortable enough to tell Wendy her feelings, Wendy would have known what the problem was. She and Charlotte could have talked about it and found mutually satisfying ways to solve it. Charlotte would not have withdrawn from the family feeling lonely and unwanted. And certainly she would not have become depressed. Most important, the process of solving it openly and mutually would have brought them emotionally closer.

That Mother was not willing to say what was in her heart may have been caused by the old family rule that "parents are supposed to be strong and not tell their children their troubles." Many parents cling to this notion as an essential component of the definition of parent. In other words, for a parent to be a "parent" or at least a "successful" parent, she must always demonstrate to her "child" a façade of having it all together—of being in perfect control. Such a pose generally does not work for elderly parents, who need emotional support from their children—especially when they and their children live under the same roof. In daily proximity, parents and adult children living together must communicate their troubling emotions in order to maintain harmony and closeness.

Children can also get stuck in a maze of old, irrelevant patterns. "That children should *never* get angry at their parents" seems to be the rule that causes the thorniest problems in the context of the relationship between the adult child and the elderly parent. Yet, in all intimate relationships where there is love there is anger. Certainly, living with parents, seeing and interacting with them on a daily basis cannot always be sweetness and light. Occasions will arise when a grown child will get angry at her elderly parent. Anger can be provoked in a child by something as simple as a parent telling that child she spends too much money on clothing. Anger of a more shameful and subtle nature may also be caused by annoyance over a parent's physical or mental decline. Remember that anger is as normal as joy or happiness. Suppressing anger, not allowing its expression, strains the bond between parent and child and may even affect the health of both parties. Moreover, the acknowledgement of anger by either party is a clear sign of trouble in the relationship, indicating a need to find out what is wrong and how to bring resolution.

One of the major stumbling blocks to clear, forthright communication between parent and child is the misunderstanding of the concept of role reversal. Though discussed more fully in Chapter 5, its message bears repeating: parents never become their children's children, no matter how frail or dependent they become. Communicating to one's parent as though that parent were a child not only demeans the parent but prevents the development of the honesty and openness necessary to closeness and harmony. At this stage in the development of the family, communication between the generations takes place on a different level. The earlier dynamic of "parent" to "child" yields to "adult" to "adult" where respect for each other's needs and wishes is the governing factor in negotiating conflicts.[4]

To help elderly parents and grown children maintain harmony through open communication, we suggest setting aside time every week or every other week for "talk times." Twice a month, however, is a bare minimum. Resentments allowed to build up over a longer period become difficult to talk about. They may even be acted out by one or both parties in a destructive fashion. A perfect example is the case of Wendy and Charlotte discussed earlier. Wendy withdrew from her family rather than talk about what troubled her. In doing so she eventually endangered her health.

How often "talk time" sessions ought to be scheduled and how long they ought to last can be spelled out in the living-together agreement described in Chapter 6. When "talk times" are held on a regular basis and become part of the family system, parties know they *must* talk. Because they must talk, they can talk.

Talk-times might be held after dinner with coffee and dessert or on a weekend afternoon or evening. Family members must select a time when everyone can be present and when everyone feels relaxed. These talk-times can be viewed as family support groups, where members feel safe in verbalizing whatever bothers them. The purpose of talk-times is to bring all troubling emotions and feelings to the surface and find mutually satisfying ways to resolve conflicts over differing needs, values, and viewpoints. Over a period of time, family members will feel at ease asserting their wishes. With practice, they will learn how to handle problematic situations fairly and kindly, with respect for one another's sensibilities. A son, for example, who was unable to work in his study because his mother played the TV too loudly, could say to her. "Mom, I know how much you love to watch TV in the family room. But some nights I really have important work to get done, and the sound comes through to my study. I would be so grateful if on those nights you could watch in your own room. How would you feel about that? Or do you have other suggestions about how we can work this out?" Or a mother might say to her daughter: "I know you think you're helping me by making my bed. Sometimes I do want your help, but I really like to take care of my room myself. Please ask me next time, before you decide to do something for me—I'd appreciate that."

Knowing they will not be judged or demeaned for what they have to say, parents and children feel good about themselves in these sessions. They likewise feel enormous relief from having expressed emotions, which bottled-up have the potential to cause stress with its resultant unhealthy physical effects. Nurturing rather than threatening, talk-sessions are therapeutic and certainly cost less than visits to a mental health professional. The ultimate goal of talk-sessions, of course, is the achievement of family closeness and lessening of isolation for the parent.

To develop the safe, nonjudgmental atmosphere required for talk-times, certain rules are helpful. These rules form the basis of all open and honest communication among individuals. They respect the differences that make us fully human. Although they allow the expression of all feelings, from joy to anger and despair, they do not permit statements that cause hurt and pain.

Communication Rules for Talk-Times

1. *The person who is talking must be allowed to finish what she is saying without interruption.* The temptation to complete

sentences and thoughts of others can be strong. Most of us are not aware of how often we do this. The urge to interrupt is especially powerful when conversing with older individuals, who perhaps speak more slowly and haltingly. To speak for anyone but particularly an older person is to deprive that person of control and her identity. Speaking for another or interrupting demeans that person. Such behavior says: "You don't count. You don't know what you're talking about. I can say it better."

2. *The person or persons who are listening must learn to listen nondefensively.* Whatever the person who is communicating says is an expression of her feelings and thoughts at that particular time. She deserves to be fully heard without the listener rushing in to defend herself against what is being said. "I'm not that way at all; you've got it all wrong; give me a chance to explain and tell my side" are nonproductive responses. Nondefensive listening is necessary if family members are to feel safe expressing whatever is on their minds. They know their thoughts and feelings will be respected and accepted for exactly what they are—expressions of self at that moment, neither designed nor spoken to inflict hurt.

3. *The person or persons who are listening must avoid statements that "invalidate" what someone is saying.* *Validating* another's feelings goes a step further than nondefensive listening. It requires of the listener active responses that indicate to the talker that what she feels is "okay" and that she likewise is okay. "I can understand how hard that must be for you; what a time you must be having; I'm happy to finally learn how you feel" are all validating statements. "I don't understand, Mother, how you can say you are depressed, when we go out of our way to make you part of all family activities" is an *invalidating* statement. Say rather, "I am sorry to hear you are feeling depressed and neglected and let us see what we can do about it." Such a statement acknowledges Mother's right to feel as she does and additionally makes Mother feel good about herself—the words do not demean; rather they enhance her feelings of self-worth.

4. *The person who is speaking must learn to use "I" statements when expressing thoughts and feelings.* "I" statements are neither accusatory nor hurtful; they are merely expressions of

what that person is feeling at a particular time. "You" statements have the power to blame and to hurt. "I feel unneeded lately because I haven't been able to help with household chores" is more effective than "You won't let me do a thing; you make me feel useless." Or "Dad, I really get angry when you tell me how to manage my accounts" is healthier than "Dad, you have a way of making me feel like a child again with your constant criticisms." Avoid statements that blame—"you're wrong; you made me get angry; you should not have done that; you made me act that way."

5. *Both the person talking and the persons listening must learn to understand the power of touch when communicating.* Using touch to reinforce communication may be difficult for some adult children, but touch has the power to generate feelings of closeness, validation, and empathy. Many people erroneously believe that the elderly no longer require physical contact. Nothing could be further from the truth! All human beings want to be touched and held. The elderly especially yearn for physical closeness since their other senses have begun to fail them. Holding Mom's hand during an emotional moment in a "talk-time" session conveys to her that her child is really there for her. Also, never underestimate the power of saying, "I like you and want to be close to you" with a good, warm hug.

Families for whom talk sessions may be initially awkward and who are confused about how to begin and what to say may be helped by a few pointers. Someone, perhaps the adult child, might want to start a session by asking her parent what, if anything, has troubled or upset her over the past week. Or the adult child might want to begin on a positive note by telling her parent how much she appreciates her preparing dinner last night. Another positive opener might be, "What has happened since our last 'talk-time' that has really made you feel good about our living together?" Talk-times need not only be gripe sessions. The purpose of talk-times is to air everything—from joy and happiness to despair and anger.

The content and spirit of any talk-time is determined by what family members bring to it. Often a family member might want to talk about something that has happened outside the family—at work or with a friend. Events occurring outside the family system can and do impinge upon what is going on within the family and bear discussion. A teenage granddaughter, for example, told her live-in grandfather, who complained about her "shortness" with him that "what with rehearsals for the school play and problems I'm having with my boyfriend, I can't be so nice to you when I return from school." A son who was experiencing pressures on the job felt it necessary to talk about his situation because the extra quiet time he needed at home was interpreted by his mother as rejection of her.

In essence, the parent becomes a "dependent" when she moves into an adult child's home and consequently is insecure and uncertain about what role to play. To keep the harmony, the adult child must reach out more than halfway. Even the most confident and secure parent is reluctant to overstep boundaries. Most elderly parents are uncomfortable asking for help or a simple favor. They are afraid of being a burden or "making trouble." When living in her adult child's house, the pressure on Mom to make as few waves as possible, to be neither seen nor heard, is intense. To be a "dependent" means uncertainty and confusion. One mother who lives with adult children said: "Frequently I feel as if I'm walking around on tiptoes. My children are so busy with their jobs and other responsibilities that I just don't want to be in their way. Sometimes when I have problems that I want to talk about, I feel they are not really interested. Sometimes I feel they don't care or don't have time to care about my life."

Alienation of this nature is physically and emotionally harmful. Merely living with others does not produce a sense of belonging. Some adult children believe that just having Mom move will automatically solve all her problems: Mom will be happier and less lonely. She will always feel wanted. Not so! Parents must be *made* to feel part of the family by their adult children. The adult child in whose home Mother lives must take the major share of responsibility for Mother's happiness.

Of course, some parents can never be happy—not because they are elderly but because the capacity for happiness was never there to begin with. These parents referred to in Chapter 5 as "succorance-seekers" are always searching for others to fill needs that can never be filled. When these parents move in, the odds for a successful living arrangement are minimal if not zero. The parents we speak of here are essentially responsible, loving persons. Because of the limitations and uncertainties attendant with being a "dependent," they naturally need encouragement and support in making the transition from living where they are fully in control to living with their children where they are not. We are not advocating some kind of co-dependent relationship between parent and child. We are only urging the adult children to understand the real problems parents have when they move in. Keeping the harmony means extra work for adult children. Reaching out to Mother by letting her know that you would like to have her company at a particular time or you would enjoy a cup of tea with her before bed time sends a clear message that she is, indeed, a vital part of the family. These gestures tell her that she does belong.

If the elderly parent is healthy and has a high level of functioning, the uncomfortable feeling of "dependent" can be reduced by finding meaningful ways for that parent to be useful in the home. A harmonious household depends on a parent achieving that sense of really contributing to the operation of the household. An eighty-five-year-old father who has been living with his son and daughter-in-law for two years told us with great pride how much his family needs him: "From the time my son was a little boy he was never interested in learning how to use tools or in fixing things. I hang pictures, repair broken towel bars, build shelves for my grandchildren's rooms, and even refinish furniture. My daughter-in-law thinks I'm the greatest and tells me this all the time. I feel just wonderful living here; I feel as if this is really my home." Another mother, seventy-three, who has been living with her daughter's family for three years boasts: "I am an important part of this household. Without me, certain things would not get done, and my daughter would not be able to work. I baby-sit my eight-year-old grandson, I prepare meals, do all the sewing—why everyone would be wearing clothes without buttons if it weren't for me—and most of the laundry. I am not unhappy here. From the very beginning, my daughter and her husband let me know that I was not only wanted but needed."

Whenever possible, and certainly if a parent is mentally intact, she should be allowed and encouraged to make decisions and choices about whatever affects her life. The adult child must not usurp extra powers because her parent is now on her territory. On the contrary, she must be sensitive to Mother's heightened feelings of dependency and foster her autonomy even in seemingly unimportant matters. A daughter told one of the authors how at one time she would always pressure her mother to join in certain outings even when Mother clearly did not wish to participate. At the urging of her sixteen-year-old son, who as an adolescent could identify with his grandmother's aversion to being pushed and her need for space, she stopped infantilizing her mother, allowing her to stay home if this was her wish. In this instance, wisdom came from the youngest generation!

Another daughter stopped making breakfast for her father every morning, when she realized that her doing so only added to his feelings of dependency. As she tells it, "One morning the full meaning of what I was doing hit me. So, I said to my Dad, 'You're on your own, from now on.' He just beamed."

Elderly parents, and the elderly in general, need to talk about the past. This reminiscence is part of a larger looking-back process called *life review*. Robert Butler, chairman of the department of Gerontology at Mount Sinai Hospital and Medical School in New York City, defines life review as a "naturally occurring, universal mental process characterized by the progressive return to consciousness of past experiences and particularly the resurgence of unresolved conflicts."[5] By recovering memories, both hurtful and gratifying, the elderly individual comes to terms with who she is and the experiences and events that shaped her identity. Life review is a healing process whose impetus is approaching death. By talking about past struggles and hardships as well as triumphs and achievements, parents are able to bring meaning to their currently limited, often painful lives. Reminiscence is how the elderly make sense out of this mystery we call life; it enables them to find meaning and purpose in the years they have lived.

We advise adult children, when they have the emotional energy for active listening, to encourage reminiscence in their parents. If a parent has the urge to reminisce at what may be an inconvenient time for the adult child, the adult child must reassure her parent that she *does* wish to listen and plan for another more appropriate time to do so. In no way should a parent be allowed to perceive a child's inability to listen to a retelling of significant life experiences as rejection. One son-in-law, whenever he has the energy to listen, loves to usher Mom to a quiet place where she can talk about and he can avidly absorb tales of her life growing up in a small town on the Adriatic coast of Italy. He claims that after these very intimate encounters Mom's mood is elevated and that she is easier to get along with. His motivation for listening and "being there," however, is not manipulative. He genuinely delights in what she has to say.

Life review is also a meaningful way for children to learn about those forces and experiences that shaped their parents' identities. Finding out about a parent before she became a parent rounds out the adult child's identity as well. Often too, life review clarifies why a parent is the way she is and the nature of a particular parent-child relationship. Its benefits may even extend to the next generation. One daughter whose father lived with her relates that after her father spoke of how hard it was for him growing up as the eldest of seven children in a family where his own father died when he was twelve, she was able to appreciate his strong opinions about money, family responsibility, and loyalty. She was able to use the knowledge learned from her father's reminiscences to help her seventeen-year-old son deal more compassionately with his grandfather's constant criticism of the way he spent his allowance.

As a component of the process of life review, reminiscence is to be encouraged. It is not only healing for parents but also may create new levels of intimacy between the generations. If a parent's stories become repetitive and the adult child can no longer bear to hear them, then ask someone else to listen. An adult daughter whose talkative, albeit interesting father has lived with her for three years includes him in dinner parties and visits with friends, where his tales are met with an enthusiasm she can no longer muster.

Another facet to reminiscence that warrants attention is that it offers a meaningful way for a parent to transmit wisdom and values from one generation to the next. As parents age, the role of parent shifts from the earlier definition of protector and nurturer to sage and teacher. For the parent who becomes a dependent in his child's home and is uncertain about his "place" in this new situation, the role of transmitter of wisdom feels right. At a time when a parent's world and power shrink because of physical, social, and economic losses, the title of "wise person" or "wise head" empowers her and enhances her self-esteem. Of course, if a parent feels good about herself, she will feel good about where and with whom she lives.

The developmental tasks of parents and middle-aged children are dramatically different and beg understanding if intergenerational harmony is to be sustained. The aging parent is adjusting to decreasing physical strength and declining health while his middle-aged child is approaching the threshold of awareness of waning physical abilities. The aging parent is adjusting to retirement with concomitant loss of income while his middle-aged child is grasping at final opportunities to succeed in career or job. The aging parent may be adjusting to loss of spouse while his middle-aged child may be reevaluating his marriage in terms of bringing new life to it or considering separation and divorce. The aging parent is actively engaged in finishing old business in preparation for death while his middle-aged child is just beginning to feel the stirrings of his own mortality.

With parent and child under the same roof, the differences in tasks may manifest themselves in seemingly unresolvable conflicts in values. The compulsion to stay fit and trim in today's body-oriented society may elicit criticism, jealousy, and anger from a parent with physical infirmities. Rushing out the door to aerobics or tennis while Mother remains at home may be perceived by Mother as frivolous and uncaring. Mother cannot understand why her daughter or son should pursue such activities rather than spend a quiet evening with her in the living room. Likewise a parent may be critical of her fifty-year-old daughter's strong involvement in her career. As an irate mother told us: "My daughter has been in Russia now for a week doing business for her firm. I don't like it one bit. I don't understand why she has to do all these things but I know I must accept her for how and what she is. Every time she leaves the house on one of her trips, I am angry. She knows it, and it is a matter of contention between us."

One daughter whose mother, recently widowed, moved in with her husband and her recalls how difficult the living situation became when she and her husband were experiencing serious marital problems. She says the following: "My husband and I were not only arguing a great deal but he was spending lots of time away from home. Although we were going to marriage counseling sessions, we felt we were not being helped. Eventually we separated. My mother, who had just lost her husband, my father, could not fathom why anyone should have marriage problems. After all, if she and my father were married for forty-five years, why couldn't my husband and I make it? She additionally blamed me for all our problems. It was a terrible time for both Mother and me. We went to counseling, and it took a year for Mother to understand why I wanted to be alone. Here we were: she without a spouse by accident; I without a spouse by choice."

The converse is also likely in that middle-aged married children may decide to pump new life into their marriage by spending more time with each other and doing more things together. They may also, in a positive vein, as part of reevaluating their marriage decide that each partner needs more space to pursue individual interests. Either way, the parent who lives at home may feel left out, uncared for, and resentful.

Not enough can be said about the different approaches to the topic of death between the elderly and the middle-aged. Elderly parents are poignantly aware of the finiteness of their days. Although those elderly who have lived their lives fully are neither preoccupied with nor fear death, they do give it serious thought and most are more than willing to share their feelings on the matter. Today, especially, in a technological age that can prolong life without quality and where living wills are fast becoming a realistic option, knowledgeable elderly have strong convictions about how they wish to die. Most middle-agers, on the other hand, are uncomfortable when "death" is brought up and prefer to avoid the matter. The closest they come to acknowledging their own eventual demise is that they know they must squeeze as much as they can into their healthy middle years. As they witness death and serious illness in their peers, however, they may become painfully anxious about the fragility of those middle years.

Those children whose parents live with them, however, have a different concept of time. In the most graphic sense possible, from observing the physical changes in their parents, they are in complete touch with their mortality. This keen awareness, though positive when it fosters a deeper appreciation of life's brief opportunities, may also produce torment, anger, and depression. Although such feelings are appropriate, they can spill over into daily interactions, affecting the harmony of the family. Professional counseling is usually quite helpful to the adult child who is experiencing this inner turmoil. It will also enable the adult child to engage in meaningful dialogue with his parent not only about the emotions that surround death but also about how a parent wishes to be remembered.

Children living with those emotionally dependent parents described in Chapter 5 as "succorance-seekers" are also advised to get help. Help, in the form of counseling or a support group for Children of Aging Parents (CAPS) will reduce the guilt and sense of powerlessness felt by the adult child in the midst of intimidating parental forces to be a "good" daughter or son. With support and an outlet for the expression of troubling emotions, the adult child will be able to deal more effectively with a parent's demands and assaults.

With insight and knowledge into basic differences in developmental needs, parent and child have a better understanding of each other's struggles. As a result, each can develop genuine empathy for the other's thoughts and behaviors. Keeping the harmony becomes a more informed process when every difference in opinion or criticism is not construed as a personal attack.

In every successful situation of parents and children living together, both generations unequivocally and emphatically say: "It can be done, but it takes work!" Both state the necessity for honest expression of needs of all family members and for flexibility and openess to change. Happy families develop in an atmosphere where family members feel safe to be who they are and to say what ever is on their minds.

We believe and the adult children interviewed agree that because of the sensitive nature of a parent's position in her child's home, the adult child must do the greater part of the reaching out. The importance of imparting to the parent in both word and action that she does belong and is a part of the family cannot be overemphasized. Finding useful ways for a parent to contribute to the household and letting that parent know she is still valued for her advice and wisdom reinforce the sense of belonging necessary to keep the harmony. Parents must likewise be given the opportunity to be part of all decisions that affect their lives.

Those who work at making it work describe a shared household as one of the most rewarding experiences in their lives. When the sand in the hour glass begins to run low for both generations, bringing a poignant appreciation of the shortness of life, making each moment count can become exhilarating and noble. There is no time for control or petty disagreements, only for increased mutual understanding and love.

Children talk about the special closeness that comes from living intimately with a parent on an adult basis. Grandchildren forever cherish memories of living with loving grandparents and speak of the important role they played in their development. For parents, living with their children in friendship means they have somehow done a good job of raising them.[6] Moreover, the warmth and love given them by their children in their later years eclipse all earlier expressions of filial devotion.

Support from the Outside

Description of Community Resources That Can Be Helpful to Shared Households

A successful shared living arrangement may also involve using available community resources to either sustain or enrich this arrangement. Most states and municipalities offer a wide variety of programs and services to help maintain the elderly in the community. Although your own town may not have all of these resources, it is important to find out what is available to assist you and your parent in living together. The adult child does not have to prove that she is a "superwoman" by supplying total care for her parent. The more she can plug into the community social service network for concrete services, the more energy and time she will have for the emotional support to the parent. The use of formal resources can help reduce the burden on the adult child and improve the quality of the care for the parent and the relationship between the generations.

As we discussed in Chapter 3, the best place to begin to explore the services and programs for the elderly that exist in your community is the area agency on aging or the state unit on aging. Most of these agencies have a toll-free hotline for information and referral. Chapter 3 also describes a number of different programs that offer companionship and friendly visiting. The example we discussed was the Home Friends Program. Even if the daughter is not working and is at home, her parent may need some additional socializing particularly if she is homebound.

Transportation and escort service, another excellent source of assistance for the caregiver was also mentioned in Chapter 3. The use of these services relieves the adult child of having to be her parent's chauffeur and reduces some of the dependency of the parent on the child.

Two other programs, telephone reassurance and emergency response systems, that make older people living alone feel more secure can also be helpful in two-generation shared households. Here again these measures are essential when the parent is frail or ill and adult children are working; however, they also serve a useful purpose for the nonworking adult child when she has to be away from the home for any length of time.

For the ambulatory older parent who lives in her child's home it may be important to develop new social contacts, particularly if she is alone for most of the day and her present living arrangement is located far from her former neighborhood. Nutrition programs and senior centers are excellent solutions to this problem.

Nutrition sites are federally subsidized programs and have been in existence since the early 1970s. They are located in a variety of places, such as housing projects, YMCAs, schools, senior centers, and other public buildings. They are open to all elderly and offer a hot noontime meal free of charge. Participants are asked to make a small donation if they can afford it.

Pamela, a seventy-seven-year-old widow, lives with her daughter and son-in-law. Both of them work, and she does not manage well when left alone. She is often depressed and has an arthritic condition. Her doctor felt that being out among people would improve both her physical and emotional state. Her daughter contacted the local area agency on aging and was referred to a nearby nutrition site. Her mother not only receives a noonday meal but participates in group activities where she meets and interacts with other older people. Since she does not drive, she also gets transportation to and from the site. She attends the program twice a week and has made a few new friends. One of them now takes her shopping once a week.

At one nutrition site we visited there were about thirty people in attendance sitting at four tables. They were chatting away and appeared to be having a good time. Most of the participants were eager to discuss how they felt about this program. One man said, "I'm single. I get a darned good meal and I don't have to cook."

Another offered, "The cooking is good and it only costs $1.50. I get good food and good companionship."

A single woman said, "I meet very good friends here and I love to hear the gossip."

"It's something to do. It breaks up the day."

"I like to meet everyone and have somebody to talk to."

In general the feeling of most of the older people was that this was an important daily activity since it provided a well-balanced, nutritious meal and an opportunity to meet and talk with a number of different people each day. As one woman put it, "It gets you out in circulation." Nutritions programs generally help replace friends who have died or moved away.

Some senior centers participate in the federal nutrition program. This type of facility usually offers a more comprehensive package of services and activities and is open for a full day. In many communities the senior center functions as the major resource for all the elderly in that locality. In Chapter 7 we saw how Josie's mother, Marie, finally accepted going to a senior center and the difference this made in both their lives.

Sally, a long-time widow who was eighty-seven years old, had become very depressed, stopped eating, and spent most of the day in bed. She had been living with her divorced daughter who worked full time. Her daughter got her dressed and gave her breakfast each morning but Sally was alone for the rest of the day. Her eyesight had begun to deteriorate, and her daughter-in-law had been very ill. Having been an unusually outgoing and active person involved in community organizations, she now could not handle the two crises in her life.

Sally was encouraged to attend a senior center, which has made a significant difference in her mental outlook. Finding friends at the center who care about her, and taking pleasure in being a helper, she thoroughly enjoys all center programs, including participation in a fashion show. The center staff always make sure that she goes on all their trips and call her in advance to remind her.

Her center is open seven days a week and serves breakfast as well as lunch. On weekends, the center shows feature films, runs bingo games, and serves lunch or a substantial snack. Transportation is also provided on weekends. The center averages between 75 and 125 participants during the week and attracts at least 100 on weekends. Like many other such facilities, it functions as a multipurpose center with social events, crafts, a speaker's program, parties, and other entertainment. It also offers a dial-a-ride service to and from doctors, dentists, hospitals, and social agencies in town and in neighboring communities, and runs a minibus for shopping and other errands.

A typical week's program at a large urban center consists of ceramics, memory class, chair exercise, Spanish conversation, social line dancing, games, drawing and painting, sewing, social action, drama, recycling, bridge, exercise-dancing, crafts, piano and song, knitting and crocheting, hair care, discussion, chorus, folk dance, and bingo. Special programs for a typical month include films, a membership meeting, a lecture on local history, a play, and a birthday party.

According to one senior center director, a center serves as a focal point for the elderly and provides access to services in a nonthreatening manner. "It keeps their support system alive and well, and in a positive way it fills the voids caused by the many losses they experience. Best of all, a senior center helps older people remain independent and in control of their lives." Both nutrition programs and senior centers serve the elderly who live with adult children as well as those who live alone.

Adult day care is available for the less mentally competent, the physically handicapped, or the socially deprived elderly. These programs usually operate five days a week for a full day and offer both medical and social supportive services. They provide meals and transportation. Many of these centers are subsidized by nonprofit agencies; the services at subsidized centers are free or cost a minimal amount. Private adult day care agencies charge a daily fee.

A typical day care center in an urban area offers both medical and social day care services, including recreation, hot meals, transportation, counseling, health screening, supervision of medications, treatments as prescribed by the doctor, physical, speech, and occupational therapies, family education and support, and assessment and case management.

One such day care center, housed in its own building, is sponsored by a nonprofit religious organization. It has an enrollment of seventy-seven people and an average daily attendance of forty-five. It is an attractive facility with one very large community room, a number of smaller crafts and card rooms, and a kitchen. The spaces are bright and cheerful; the place hums with activity. At large and small tables throughout the center, groups of people sit and talk. Some play dominoes and other games; some read; some do crafts; and some paint. The groups look animated and the people appear to be having a good time.

The center is open five days a week from 8 A.M. to 4 P.M. and serves breakfast, lunch, and snacks. A flexible schedule enables those who prefer it to come later in the morning or to attend just two or three days a week. In addition to the medical services available at the center, people needing special rehabilitation and physiotherapy are transported to a nearby hospital. A few times a year special trips and picnics are scheduled. When the weather permits, the participants are taken to a park where they can walk or just contemplate nature. Special events and parties are scheduled for holidays. Elementary and high school students visit from time to time and interact with the older people. At Halloween, they come dressed in costumes and play games at the center.

This center is free for low-income elderly. For those who can afford it, the fee is $30 a day, including transportation. Participants range in age from fifty-five to ninety-two.

Sybil, eighty-two, has been coming to the center for over a year. Widowed for more than forty years, she lives with her only son. An outgoing and attractive person who led a quiet life centered around friends and church activities, she was able to live in her own home until her stroke two years ago, which left her weakened on her left side. Although, if aided, she can walk a few steps, she is essentially confined to a wheelchair.

Her son was willing to have her move into his home but only if she agreed to attend a day care center on a regular basis. Sybil said that when it was explained to her, "it sounded like an old folk's home and I wouldn't have any of that." She resisted until the center director visited her a few times and encouraged her to come on a trial basis. After about a week, Sybil decided that she really liked it and has been a regular participant ever since.

Sybil is an outgoing person and has made many friends. "We get along real good," she said. "I just enjoy myself. Something is always going on. And talking to people all the time makes me very happy." In addition to visiting with her friends at the center, she enjoys the classes in writing and drawing, the poetry recitals, the group singing, and the twice-a-week church services where they sing hymns. She also participates in the kitchen activities in the afternoons when a small group prepares vegetables and other food for the next day's meals.

Adult day care centers serve the frail elderly and help maintain or restore their maximal functional abilities. A growing need for this type of facility seems to be matched by the rapid growth of these programs. In 1978, there were 300 adult-care centers in the country in forty states, serving over 5,000 people. Today 2,000 centers in all the states serve over 70,000.[1]

Angels of mercy in the guise of certified home health aides are perhaps the backbone of home health care in America. Extensively trained by nurses and other professionals in the special medical, psychological, and social needs of the elderly, they are available to give beleaguered caregivers help with personal care, laundry, shopping, meal preparation, and light housekeeping. Home health aides free the adult child to do some of the things she did before Mom moved in. The working daughter mentioned at the end of Chapter 5 who manages to play tennis almost every day and keep her Friday appointment with the hairdresser utilizes the services of home health aides. One aide appears every morning at eight to bathe, toilet, and feed Mom so that her daughter can go to her job. She stays until one, when another aide appears, who cares for Mom until daughter returns home. Since Daughter often comes home late, as she plays tennis after work, the aide will prepare a light evening meal for the family. Although these services are expensive, Daughter says they are well worth the cost, as they prevent her from feeling resentful or angry over the disruptions caused by Mom's presence.

Although home health care is a rapidly growing industry in America, there is still a shortage of these important personnel. Often too, it may be hard to find someone whom Mom will immediately like. Most agencies, however, are accommodating, doing their utmost to make a good match between client and aide. Since aides are highly trained in understanding the elderly and those selected are carefully screened for maturity and compassion, they are sensitive to clients' fears and vulnerabilities.

Home health care agencies can be found in the yellow pages of any telephone book. They are listed under "Home Health Services." Many insurance plans, including Medicare, Medicaid, and Blue Cross/Blue Shield, pay for home care services upon discharge from a hospital. For those individuals whose insurance does not completely cover needed home health care services, agencies like the Visiting Nurse Association offer a sliding scale for certain services.

The Visiting Nurse Association and many home health agencies also provide skilled nursing care. From monitoring high-tech medical equipment to inserting a catheter, to measuring blood pressure, registered nurses are available to make home visits. Although insurance usually covers most of these skilled services, it is best to ask beforehand what services are eligible for reimbursement.

When looking for a home health aide, you must find out if the agency meets state and federal standards of accreditation. Those that meet federal criteria can accept reimbursement through Medicare and Medicaid. Do not hesitate to ask questions about insurance coverage and fees. Although fees do not vary significantly, a dollar or two can make a difference when many hours of care are required.

"Meals on Wheels," the most common name for the many at-home meal services offered to homebound elderly, can make a big difference to caregivers who work and whose parents are too frail or disabled to prepare a well-balanced meal. Home-delivered meals may be sponsored by the Red Cross, the Visiting Nurse Association, local hospitals, Nutrition Sites, or other nonprofit organizations. Funding for these vital services comes from title 3 of the Older Americans Act. Although each meal costs only a moderate amount, the older person who cannot afford the cost may pay whatever she can each week. No one is ever denied a meal because of inability to pay. Area offices on aging or social service departments of hospitals provide information on "Meals On Wheels" programs.

Mental health services for caregivers and/or their parents are available at community mental health centers or family service agencies throughout the country. Staffed mainly by qualified social workers, most counseling agencies today have programs to help individuals and families who are having problems related to caring for aging parents. Family service agencies, for example, offer counseling (individual, family, and group), psychotherapy, care management, crisis intervention, and home visits for assessment and future planning. Marcy and Tom (see Chapter 10) whose marriage was strained by Tom's manipulative mother sought help from a family service agency. Since the shared household, with its diverse cast of characters, is fertile soil for relationship problems, it is imperative that families not only know of available mental health services but use them as soon as troublesome rumblings are heard.

In addition to all the services available to older people, most communities offer volunteer and employment opportunities as well. Action, a federal agency, administers several volunteer programs through local grantees: among them are the Foster Grandparent Program (FGP), Senior Companion Program (SCP), and Retired Senior Volunteer Program (RSVP). The first two, FGP and SCP, offer low-income people aged sixty and over the chance to work twenty hours a week for a small stipend, with expenses paid and the added benefit of an annual physical examination. Trained and supervised by sponsoring agencies (schools, hospitals, day care centers) foster grandparents serve four hours per day tending the needs of mentally and physically handicapped children. Volunteers in the SCP assist homebound, chronically disabled elderly; indeed, delivery of many in-home services depends on these older volunteers.

RSVP, which has no income limits, serves a variety of organizations.

Volunteer stations may include courts, schools, libraries, day care centers, hospitals, Boy Scout and Girl Scout offices, economic development agencies, and other community service centers. Volunteers are not paid, but they may be reimbursed for transportation, meals, and other out-of-pocket expenses connected with their service. They receive a brief orientation from the local RSVP project director and in-service instruction after placement.

For some of the elderly, earning money may be a more urgent matter than keeping busy or being of service. But finding a job is difficult for most older people. To help provide employment opportunities for low-income seniors who are fifty-five or older, the U.S. Department of Labor subsidizes community service projects administered by public or nonprofit agencies or organizations. Projects must contribute to the general welfare of communities as well as increase employment opportunities for older people. Some national contractors approved for funding are Green Thumb (an affiliate of the National Farmers Union), American Association of Retired Persons (AARP), National Council on the Aging (NCOA), and the U.S. Forestry Service. NCOA, for example, provides work and training opportunities for approximately ten thousand older persons each year.[2]

A service that provides specific help to the adult child is provided by employers who recognize that many of their employees are caregivers for their parents and need help in maintaining their dual roles. Currently, only a small number of companies provide some form of "eldercare" assistance to their workers. This benefit however, will become popular as more employers become aware of their employees' reduced effectiveness due to the stress of caregiving. The types of eldercare services provided range from dissemination of information to referral and counseling service to arranging on-site day care for elderly parents to liberal leave policies and flexible work options for caregivers.[3]

Respite care is one of the most important services that can help relieve the adult child temporarily from her caregiving responsibilities. This service consists of temporary in-facility twenty-four-hour supervision for persons who depend upon a primary caregiver for support. Nursing homes, hospitals, and rehabilitation centers are the usual sites for this type of care and allow for fifteen to thirty live-in days. Some programs are state subsidized, so that families with low- to-moderate incomes and assets can avail themselves of these vital services on a co-payment basis.

In recent years, the concept of respite care has been broadened to include medical or social care in the home as well as in a separate facility. These services may be provided on an hourly, daily, or overnight basis, not to exceed thirty consecutive days. It can include companion/sitter, chore and homemaker, personal care, and home health services. Services can be provided by trained senior companions, volunteers, homemakers, home health aides, and, when appropriate, by registered nurses or social workers.

With respite care, the adult child can take a break for a few days to a few weeks, knowing that her parent will receive competent personal and medical supervision and care. Information is available through the local office on aging or the local hospital. Just a weekend away from caregiving chores can make a considerable difference in the caregiver's attitude and disposition. Remember, caregiving is stressful and draining. As with any job, one must occasionally take a breather in order to maintain one's motivation. The penalty for this kind of self-neglect is burnout, culminating in physical or emotional illness.

Of all caregivers, adult children whose parents live with them are the most vulnerable to stress-related illness (for example, headaches, backaches, or stomach disorders). An excellent example of the powerful effect of emotions on the body was provided to us by a dermatologist. He said that among his female patients suffering from neurodermatitis (a stress-related ecxema characterized by itching, redness, and inflammation) it was not uncommon to see flare-ups in daughters whose mothers had moved in with them.

If the adult child uses the available community services, including respite care, and still experiences stress and perhaps anger toward her parent, then it is time for her to consider joining a support group for children of aging parents. A major benefit of these groups is that they afford individuals the opportunity to be with others who are experiencing similar dilemmas and emotions. We all feel much better about ourselves when we learn we are not unique in our misery; that others out there have the same unacceptable thoughts and feelings that we do.

Anger toward a parent, especially a frail, elderly one, easily falls into the category of "unacceptable feelings." Those harboring this emotion irrationally believe they are "bad" daughters who have failed to achieve proper filial respect. After all, the mandate to honor thy father and mother does not include a clause saying it is okay to be angry at them for getting old or for making demands upon our lives, or for constantly reminding us that soon we will be where they are. Given the cultural taboo against expressing anger, is it any wonder that the adult child involved in giving care to an elderly parent would rather bottle it up than give vent to it? At a support group meeting listening to others spew similar rage and reveal similar experiences, the caregiver knows that here she can tell all. Because others in the group feel as she does, she can risk self-disclosure; she will not be judged or humiliated. At best, she will receive the validation that she is still okay; that she is still a good and lovable human being.

An organization called Children of Aging Parents (CAPS) provides information and referral services throughout the country for caregivers (see appendix D). It also works to increase community awareness of the problems of aging and caregiving through educational programs, workshops, and seminars. It produces and distributes literature for caregivers and helps develop support groups for its membership throughout the country. Because CAPS provides comprehensive services to caregivers, parents and children who live together should consider it a prime resource.

His Mother, Not Hers

Examination of the Unique Problems Presented by the Parent as an In-Law

When Mother moves in with her son and daughter-in-law, the strain on the latter and on the marital system may be especially severe. Although in these instances, the son is designated the primary caregiver, he may hold this position in name only. Current research indicates that daughters-in-law actually perform the bulk of caregiving chores when their husbands' mothers move into their homes. In fact, according to Amy Horowitz of the Brookdale Center On Aging, "Men were significantly more likely to name their wives as one of the other relatives involved in providing care to their parent than were the adult daughters to report that their husbands were involved."[1] Either way, as daughters or as daughters-in-law, women appear destined by gender to assume the caregiving role.

Mothers and daughters, however, bound by blood and a long history of emotional involvement generally find caregiving less stressful. Folklore has it that a mother-in-law and a daughter-in-law in the same kitchen are like a lion and lamb in the same cage. The modern woman bluntly states it this way: "My mother and I together in the kitchen are just fine; My mother-in-law, forget it. It's pure hell!"

It only makes sense that care given from marital obligation rather than from filial obligation would be different. Daughters-in-law cannot be expected to feel as close to their husbands' mothers as to their own. The repository of love, affection, and loyalty produced by a lifetime of shared family experiences that allows mothers and daughters to say what is on their minds, to argue and disagree with one another, later forgiving and forgetting, does not exist between a mother-in-law and her daughter-in-law. A daughter, for example, can either resign herself with humor to a difficult parent's incessant demands or tell her outright to stop harassing her. A daughter-in-law, under similar conditions, may have to bite her lip or punch a few pillows. The emotional and physical toll on the daughter-in-law as a result of having to suppress her anger is incalculable. Days, months, and years of harboring troubling emotions and thoughts toward and about someone whom she sees every day and with whom she may share a kitchen or living room can and will eventually make her sick.

If the mother-in-law who shares the household is seriously disabled, requiring difficult, personal, hands-on care, *and* the historical relationship between her and her daughter-in-law has been conflictual, the caregiving situation will be fraught with unbearable stress.[2] To share a household with a mother-in-law who functions and is independent is one thing; to share a household with one who is abject and needy is quite another. Helping a mother-in-law one neither likes nor loves with personal, back-breaking tasks such as bathing, toileting, and dressing can exacerbate preexisting negative emotions. One daughter-in-law summed it up thus: "Although my mother-in-law and I never liked each other from day one, as long as we lived apart we were able to maintain a façade of cordiality. She would visit over Christmas and Thanksgiving; we would take the kids there in the summer. That was all fine, because we could say good-bye. Now, with her under the same roof and her needing me every day, there is no escape. At times I feel like a prisoner in my own home. What's worse, not that I expected it, considering our previously poor relationship, she never offers a word of thanks or the slightest recognition for all I do for her. You know, it's not easy to empty the commode every day for someone you deeply dislike. I guess what I'm feeling now is bitterness. I didn't feel that before she moved in."

Some daughters-in-law, however, tell a different story. One told us, for example, that precisely because "she is my mother-in-law, the responsibility does not weigh as heavy. I feel less burdened." As Elaine Brody points out, the desire to return to parents the total care they gave to their children does not gnaw at the daughter-in-law as it does at the daughter. Posits Brody: "They do not have the powerful motivation of reciprocity for the care they received as children or the feelings of love (albeit ambivalent) and biological connection."[3] For those daughters-in-law who are able to detach almost to the point of viewing their caregiving as a "kind of job," the tension is far less eroding to their physical and emotional well-being.

Other daughters-in-law—although we have found that these are a small minority—are fortunate to have husbands who take full responsibility for their mothers. With husbands who not only manage their mothers' finances and perform other concrete chores but also exhort them to take their medications, be more cooperative, and try to do more for themselves, these daughters-in-law are in the most optimal situation. Wives of such husbands are rarely if ever placed in the adversarial position of having to tell their mothers-in-law to do something they may not like. Although such relationships may seem cool and detached, they are, in their neutrality, polite and certainly less stressful. More important, they inflict less damage to the marital bond.

Another factor that contributes to the generally high tension in this living arrangement is the fact that Mother-in-Law and Wife sometimes compete for the attention of the Son/Husband. What Woody Allen humorously refers to as "Oedipus Wrecks" may not be quite so light when Mom and Daughter-in-Law live under the same roof. In one shared household the mother-in-law, who never thought her daughter-in-law good enough for her son, verbally abuses her daughter-in-law until her son returns from work. The moment her son comes through the door, she is sweetness and charm, pretending that all is fine. Refusing to believe his wife's horror stories about his mother's abuse, he reprimands her for her inability to be more patient and understanding with his mother. The wife told us, "I simply feel that I don't count anymore and that my mother-in-law is now in full control."

It is no wonder then that current gerontologic research has validated what women have long known to be true: mothers-in-law and daughters-in-law, by and large, cannot live under the same roof without conflict. In fact, gerontologists tell us that caregiving daughters-in-law who share households with their husbands' mothers experience more stress than any other type of caregiver.

Yet, daughters-in-law for a variety of reasons are inviting their husbands' elderly mothers to move in, and some are doing a good job of it. The story of Gail comes to mind. It illustrates not only why the decision to have Mother-in-Law move in is made but how the involved members of the family made it work. It also clearly points up the extra significance of the variable of "spousal amicability" when it's his mother, not hers.

Gail's mother-in-law, Ilene, moved in when Gail and her husband, Bruce, relocated from Chicago to Philadelphia. Prior to their relocation, Ilene had lived in her own apartment in suburban Chicago, about five miles from her son's home. In Chicago, Ilene had a small network of friends with whom she played canasta, lunched, shopped, and enjoyed a variety of other activities. When Chicago winters proved too difficult to endure, Ilene moved to Florida, returning north in the summer to be with Bruce and Gail. Spending from eight to twelve weeks in her son's home, Gail says of these summer periods, "They were in a very real sense dress rehearsals for what none of us knew was later to happen." At this time, Gail was forty, Bruce forty-three, their daughter and son fifteen and thirteen. Ilene was seventy-one. Gail relates the following story in detail, poignantly spinning out the complex themes that define this family:

"As I recall, Ilene altogether spent three summers with us. They were stressful times, to say the least. Both my children were home and though the kids would spend half the summer in day camp they still needed me for car-pooling and lots of other things. Ilene needed attention I could not give her, because I was so busy with the kids. On top of all this, my marriage was not so great and Bruce and I were in counseling. We had serious problems to work out and Mother's presence curtailed the privacy we required to talk out some of our difficulties. Our marriage counselor, in fact, prescribed that Bruce and I set aside a full hour every day to talk with each other. Ilene resented our time together, and often it seemed to Bruce and me that she really wanted to kind of sabotage us. As I look back on those days, I now realize she was doing just that. She was very competitive with me for Bruce's attention and also competitive with the kids.

"My mother-in-law, you see, is the sort of person who expects to be first. She expects to be served first at the table, even when the kids have some place to go and must be fed and out of the house. And she expects Bruce to greet her first when he comes through the door from work. I can remember a particular summer when Bruce returned from a long business trip to the Orient. We all went to pick him up at the airport and during the drive home he wanted to know all about the children and me. Much later he inquired about Ilene. Well, she became so angry and resentful that she withdrew to her room and pouted almost the entire evening. She never says she's angry, she just retreats into her shell and waits for one of us to go get her. One of us, usually me, would! That's pretty powerful manipulation.

"Knowing what a difficult, childish person Mom can be, when Bruce was transfered to Philadelphia and Mom wanted to live closer to us, I knew I could never have her move in with us. So, I did some research and found a rental retirement community not far from our home. There Mom could have her own apartment, housekeeping services, and meals if she wished. We thought this arrangement would be perfect for her—she could be independent and yet near us. But she did not like her new living arrangement and at the same time began to experience some vision problems. She fell a few times, once breaking her wrist and had difficulties administering her insulin shots.

"Five years had passed since Ilene spent summers with us in Chicago. My children were now in college, and my marriage was in great shape. I also really understood Ilene and felt I knew how to make her happy, without putting too much strain on myself. Also, and this is very important, I had a hidden agenda. One day, I knew I would want my Mom to live with us, and if I were good to Bruce's Mom, he would have to return the favor. Oddly enough, Bruce did not want his Mom to live with us. *I* pushed it, and now you can understand why.

"Actually, my relationship with Ilene is better than Bruce's. I understand her, and Bruce does not. Women are better at understanding each others' personalities and besides, I took several psychology courses in college. Ilene had a hard life; I have compassion for her. Also, I have no trouble telling Ilene how I honestly feel. That's a big advantage other daughters-in-law do not have. She may sulk when I tell her something she doesn't want to hear, but I can handle her behavior okay now. She can't put guilt trips on me anymore.

"Ilene has survived some hard times. Her first-born son died from leukemia when he was thirteen, and five years later her husband died suddenly of a heart attack. At fifty-one she was a widow with a sixteen-year-old son, Bruce, to raise and educate. She went back to work as a bank teller, put Bruce through college and graduate school, and really made a life for herself with friends and activities. I admire and respect her for what she has made of her life.

"She is, though, an unbelievably nervous person, particularly about health matters—her own health and ours and our children's. She is terrified of death, pain, and sickness and always worried that something terrible is going to happen. Of course, you can understand why she is this way, what with all the losses she has had. Bruce has trouble dealing with all her strong feelings. He finds her clinging and possessive and has no patience with me when I try to explain to him how her behavior and what she has experienced through life are connected. As an engineer, he has little time for emotional explanations and feels most people should be able to solve their problems. He's really relieved to turn her over to me.

"When Ilene pouts or goes off to her room in a huff, I know how to deal with her. I will usually go to her *once*. I tell her I understand her feelings have been hurt, that I am sorry and that it would be so much better if she would rejoin the family to talk about how she feels rather than sulk. If she chooses to remain in her room, that is her choice. Neither Bruce nor I, however, feels guilty. During those summer visits, years ago, I would continually go to her, begging her to come out. I've learned a lot since then.

"I also go out of my way to have some extremely pleasurable times with Ilene. I take her out to lunch every week. After lunch, I take her browsing through the stores. We talk about her life—her days working in the bank and what it was like for her to be widowed. We even talk about Bruce. The competition is now gone. We have a good time talking about his quirks and his rigidity. We are now allies in many ways. Through me, she has learned to better understand him; through her, I have learned important things about his childhood.

"And when my daughter and son are home, Ilene is really in her glory. They have a strong connection to one another. The children are really proud of their grandmother, and she, in turn, gives them a great deal of herself. As with all grandmothers, she loves them unconditionally.

"So, all in all, things are not so bad. I have no regrets about initiating and pushing her to move in with us. And I know that for her, though she does not say it, because it is not in her nature to give strokes, she is really happy to be part of our family during her later years. I personally feel a great sense of accomplishment in making it all work. I have grown and become a more mature, giving human being from having Ilene live with us."

Gail took a calculated risk. She knew her mother-in-law could be "difficult," but after summer "dress rehearsals" she believed she would be able to deal with her manipulations. Of note is that *Gail* wanted Eileen to move in. Planning to have her own mother live with them should it become necessary, Gail knew Bruce would be obliged to return the favor. Additionally, whereas all family systems were not stable five years earlier, they were now. Gail's and Bruce's marital problems had been worked out, and their children were no longer at home. With renewed energy, Gail was now able to devote herself more fully to Ilene's emotional and physical needs. With fewer people in the house, everyone had the luxury of more space and privacy. If ever there was a right time for Ilene to join the family, it was certainly then.

What Gail's story clearly indicates is the importance of parent and spouse amicability. Though the spouse's attitude and feelings regarding the parent's move in are always critical factors in predicting success (see Chapter 5), when it's his mother not hers, they assume extra weight. Given Bruce's dislike of his mother and his inability to let go of resentments from the past, the odds for success were not good. Gail's basic good will toward her mother-in-law and her unflagging efforts to make the shared household work made the difference.

Although Gail's relationship to her mother-in-law could not be described as close, Gail understood and respected Ilene as a person. By making a genuine effort to understand the forces that shaped Ilene's life, Gail was able to appreciate the relationship between Ilene's tragic losses and her outrageous behaviors. In a real sense, Gail became not only a buffer between Ilene and Bruce but interpreter to Bruce of the reasons behind some of his mother's actions. Eventually, because of her intense involvement with Ilene, Gail and she did become close.

In essence, Gail got along better with Ilene than Bruce did. She accepted Ilene. She dealt with her manipulations forthrightly and sensitively. Without demeaning Ilene, she let her know that certain of her behaviors were simply not acceptable. She found positives in Ilene and capitalized upon them. She valued the loving relationship Ilene had with her grandchildren and told her so. She found time to be with Ilene emotionally—to listen, to share, to reminisce with her. Gail's total demeanor conveyed to Ilene genuine interest in her as a unique human being who lived and continued to live a meaningful life. For Ilene, whose sense of self had been deeply shaken by her many losses—husband, son, job, and vision—Gail was able to give her what mattered most—the sense that she still counts.

Lest one think that Gail was a martyr in all this, she was not! Although she was tending to many of Ilene's needs, vital needs of her own were being met in the process of giving care to her mother-in-law. As she reported, she felt a "sense of accomplishment" and experienced personal growth in giving of herself to another person. Fully aware that she was the key factor in making it all work, she had a feeling of mastery and control. The real fringe benefit, however, was that having Ilene live with her strengthened her marriage to Bruce. No matter Bruce's protestations of distance from his mother; he was, nonetheless, pleased that Gail was "good" to Ilene. He also was quite candid about his sense of relief that Gail had taken the responsibility for Ilene. In caring for her mother-in-law in her home, Gail additionally, like many daughters, was insuring her right to do the same for her own mother, when and if that time should arrive. She was protecting her hidden agenda.

Of course, that the power to make decisions resided in Gail rather than Bruce only increased the chances of a successful shared household. The chain of command led directly to Gail. Since Bruce found his mother trying and preferred to avoid all conflicts with her, he allowed Gail to be in control. His peripheral role prevented him from having to be in the uncomfortable position between Wife and Mother. Gail benefited, because unlike other daughters-in-law, she felt "she came first." The usual competition for the attention of the son/husband, often considered to be natural between a mother-in-law and daughter-in-law did not exist between Gail and Ilene.

Bruce, in fact, told one of us that he was always clear about where his loyalty belonged—to Gail and his children. He went on to relate, surprising for someone purportedly out of touch with his feelings, that he felt perhaps he suffered from "survivor's guilt." He poignantly said: "When my older brother died, I felt it should have been me. I always felt that he was my mother's favorite. My strong feelings have prevented me from really being close to my mother. When I married Gail, I felt I finally had a family where I counted."

That the attitude of the daughter-in-law toward the spouse's parent is pivotal, overriding other variables governing success is borne out by Dorothy, caregiver to her husband's father. "My husband and his father never got along from day one. I know it sounds strange but they really don't like each other. That happens sometimes. My father-in-law was born in Germany and has strong feelings about what children should do for their parents. After his wife, who had taken care of him, died, he expected to move in with us. My husband wanted no part of this arrangement, but I felt we could not let his father down. Besides, money was a problem and there was no way my father-in-law could afford the care he required. He uses a walker because of stroke damage and needs help with personal care. Although I work, I knew we would be able to care for him in our house with the money he would get from selling his home. Anyway, my husband and he fight over everything from politics to how the newspaper should be folded after you're finished reading it. But my father-in-law and I get along real well. I actually like him and know how to get around him. He has been with us now for two years and things could be worse. I know that if it weren't for me my father-in-law could never live with us. Things aren't perfect and sometimes I feel like a referee separating two small boys, but it's really not so bad."

Mike, whose eighty-three-year-old mother, Rose, came to live with his wife, Linda, and him represents a more common type of shared household than Gail and Bruce's. Neither willing nor able for a variety of reasons to care for her mother-in-law, Linda required Mike's support and understanding to prevent strain in their marriage and to make Rose feel welcome in their home. Their story also illustrates the vital role of community and family resources in the context of the shared household.

Rose came to live with Mike, sixty-four, and Linda, fifty-eight, because she could no longer manage alone in her home in Philadelphia. She had become frail, her personal hygiene was poor, she was forgetting to eat, and she was having trouble walking. Additionally, her once safe ethnic neighborhood was now a dangerous place for an older woman to live. Linda and Mike decided to have Rose move in with them because they did not want to put her in a nursing home. Linda's own mother had died of complications from Alzheimer's in a nursing home two years earlier, and Linda and Mike shared negative feelings about these facilities. Besides, neither felt that Rose needed round-the-clock, skilled care.

Mike, the younger of two brothers, liked and respected his mother and felt he was the logical one to serve as primary caregiver. His older brother and wife were not only caring for their homebound, developmentally disabled daughter but Mike's brother had recently suffered a heart attack. Although Mike was retired and looking forward to more travel, golf, and tennis, he was willing to make necessary sacrifices in his leisure activities to care for his mother.

Linda, having returned to college in her late thirties to get her degree, now taught mathematics at a nearby junior high school. She loved her job and planned to work until she turned sixty-five. Concerning her relationship with her mother-in-law, Linda says: "We get along. We both respect each other though there's no great love there. We are both strong personalities. From the very beginning we clashed, and both of us learned to stay out of each other's paths. Consequently, we are polite to each other and always try to keep the conversation superficial. I do, however, respect Mike's feelings for his mom. Mike and I have a good marriage, and I want to keep it that way. We talked a lot about taking Rose in before actually doing it. Mike knew I would never quit my job to help care for his mother; I didn't do it for my own mother. Besides, one day we would need my pension and health benefits. Mike agreed to take the major share of responsibility for chores and decision making and said that whatever I could do to relieve him would be appreciated."

Mike's perspective on his mother's living with them was as follows: "I wanted Mom to live with us, especially after seeing how hard it was for Linda when her Mom was in a nursing home. I'm no fool, and Linda and I have always been open with each other, so I knew having my mother with us would be a strain on Linda. Linda and my mother are not close, so that any conflicts or problems would have to be handled by me. Since I'm retired and have more time than Linda, I can do more. But I've waited and worked hard for these years and did not intend to let taking care of my mother eat away at them. My mother is a strong, independent woman, used to having her own way. At first it wasn't easy. She would not accept any outside help, and weekends Linda and I like to go away. And then there was the problem with summers. They are the only time we can really vacation and five years ago we bought a camper. My brother had a heart attack in his sixties and who's to say that's not going to happen to me? I really want to enjoy life while I can. Well, Mom had to bend. She goes to adult day care three times a week. Weekends, when we're not home, she eats afternoon meals at my brother's home and in the mornings a neighbor comes in to help her with personal chores. In the summers, when we go away for two to three weeks at a time, she frequently eats at my brother's, gets meals-on-wheels, still goes to day care, and has personal help from a neighbor. She also has the added security of our dogs and a medic alert disc, which she wears around her neck. My single, twenty-five-year-old son who practically lives around the corner does the marketing, feeds the dogs, and visits every day."

And what does Rose have to say about all these changes in her life? "Well, it has been hard. I was a widow for twenty years and used to doing things my own way. Living with a daughter-in-law just isn't meant to be. But, I must say, Linda treats me with respect and when I can be helpful, like with folding the laundry and doing some sewing, she welcomes and appreciates my help. I don't like depending on strangers, on outsiders for help, but on the other hand, the children have to get away and live. And I'd rather be here than in some home. Always better to be with family. All my friends in Philadelphia are dead; I was alone there. So I've learned to comply—that's the word, isn't it? But there's no question that it's hard to be in your children's home when you're my age and used to being independent. The best thing about living here is that I get to see my grandchildren, who live nearby and also my two sons. I really do feel that I am part of their lives and Mike and I especially find time to have some good talks."

A cool relationship between Rose and Linda, Rose's strong sense of independence conveyed by the statement, "I'm used to doing things my own way," the possible disruption of the well-deserved leisure of their middle years, and Rose's resistance to outside help all militated against a harmonious, tension-free shared household. Because Mike was willing to shoulder most of the responsibility, their living arrangement managed to succeed. More than Mike's concrete help (marketing, shopping, taking Rose to doctors' appointments, meal preparation), his readiness to handle problem areas with Rose made the big difference. Negotiating with his mother about the necessity for outside help and asserting Linda's and his needs for vacations and recreation, Mike's adult approach convinced Rose to make changes. Linda could not have been part of such contests without causing serious damage to her marriage, her relationship with her mother-in-law, and the shared household system.

Rose's capacity for flexibility enabled her to adapt. Living with her children, though hard, had more advantages than disadvantages. Rose needed her connection to her family: she valued their love and warmth; she did not want to be alone in her house in Philadelphia; she accepted her relationship with Linda for exactly what it was; she recognized that her children had to live their own lives. Rose did not merely comply; she adapted. Compliance implies subjugation of identity with consequent feelings of depression and demoralization. Rose never lost her sense of who she was. Despite her extreme fraility and dependence, her inner strength was evident. Our first impression of Rose was of a vital woman, who in her own way, was still very much in control of her life.

Referring to the questionnaires in Chapter 5, we see four fundamental themes: (1) Mike was able to see and relate to his mother as a peer, not as a parent to be feared, and, therefore, was able to assert his life needs with confidence rather than anger; (2) Rose was flexible enough to "roll with the punches"—to make necessary shifts in attitudes and actions; (3) although Rose and Linda were cool toward each other, they were still able to respect and accept each other; and (4) both Linda and Mike respected their own needs for recreation and leisure. All considered, the odds for success were good.

The odds for success were poor in the story of Marcy and Tom.

Marcy, a thirty-eight-year-old homemaker with two preschool children, was at her wit's end when she came to one of us for counseling. Her mother-in-law, Helen, seventy-three, had moved in five months earlier, and Marcy was already angry, depressed and burnt out from her caregiving responsibilities. Marcy felt that Helen's presence had strained her marriage and reduced Tom to a child, tied to his mother rather than committed to her. Moreover, Marcy felt Tom was not emotionally available to her. The few times she tried talking to Tom about how trying it was to care for Helen, he would not listen. Responding with "you're just too sensitive" or "you're not trying hard enough to understand her," Marcy felt powerless. Additionally, they had not been out as a couple since Helen moved in. Although Tom's sister, who worked full time, offered to help out on weekends, Helen flatly refused her assistance. If Helen would not allow her own daughter to stay with her to give Marcy and Tom a break, the idea of strangers, such as professional home health aides, of course, was totally unacceptable.

Helen, who had Parkinsons's and two hip replacements, had been ordered by her doctors to do as much as she could by herself, not only to regain some physical functioning, but also to combat the depression she was experiencing. During the day, when Tom was at work, Helen refused to use her walker, insisted on meals in bed, soiled herself rather than use the commode and found any of a number of ways to be uncooperative. Performing a complete about-face upon Tom's return home, Helen fooled Tom into believing that all was well and Marcy was simply overreacting because of her dislike of Helen. Always intimidating and manipulative, Helen was now a cunning tyrant. Because she had lost significant control over her life and could not adapt to her dependencies, by making life miserable for everyone else, she was, albeit destructively, able to exert a semblance of control over her limited world.

Marcy, who had always been afraid of her mother-in-law, felt powerless. She was in a no-win situation. If she asserted herself to Helen, she risked Tom's anger and further strain on her marriage. If she allowed Helen to have her own way, she would eventually become ill herself from the strain.

Although easy solutions to complex relationship problems do not exist, individual counseling and support group sessions empowered Marcy to stand up to her mother-in-law and Tom. Counseling with *both* Marcy and Tom made a bigger difference, for Tom was helped to understand the importance of giving emotional support to Marcy and in allying with rather than against her in her efforts to persuade Helen to do what was in Helen's welfare. As a united front, Marcy and Tom were able to prevent Helen from coming between them. Tom assumed the role of spokesperson in all matters pertaining to his mother's care. Rather reluctantly, for Tom too was intimidated by Helen, he became the one to issue directives about getting out of bed, eating in the kitchen, and using the walker and the commode. When Marcy complained about Helen's lack of cooperation, Tom, not Marcy, told Helen he would brook no nonsense. With Tom responsible, Marcy was no longer the "heavy." Tom ultimately told Helen she would not only have to accept Tom's sister's offers of help but the services of community resources.

With Tom's support, Marcy was under less stress, and the marital bond was considerably strengthened. The utilization of outside help likewise made a big difference in Marcy's life. For Helen, unfortunately, things did not improve. Although more cooperative, she remained angry and inconsolable. Dependency upon others, particularly her children, exacerbated her feelings of loss of control and seemed to throw her into further depression. A sad and trying era came to an end, when six months later, after minimal progress in her total level of functioning, Helen was placed in a nursing home.

The crucial factors determining success were lacking here. First, Tom, who was not sufficiently grown up to relate to his mother on an adult to adult basis, still perceived her as a powerful parent to be feared. Second, Tom's spouse, Marcy, did not like her mother-in-law and, like Tom, was intimidated by her. Third, Helen's need to be in control and her inability to accept dependency rendered her incapable of adapting to the painful changes in her life. Helen's rigidity, which extended to her refusal to accept any outside help, including her own family, exacerbated Marcy's burnout and produced further strain on a marriage already in need of help.

When *his* mother moves in, perhaps the most important factor is the willingness of husband and wife to work extra hard to sustain the couple bond. Without a united front, a manipulative and difficult mother like Helen can seriously damage a marriage. One mother-in-law always played her son and daughter-in-law against each other by detouring significant requests through the son. As the daughter-in-law told us: "When my mother-in-law wants something from us like being included in our time-out-alone shopping excursions, she never asks me but him. In the beginning Bob would always agree assuming it would be okay with me. For a long time I went along with this, getting more and more boiled up inside. When I finally got up enough courage to tell him what was happening, he put an immediate stop to her manipulations. He told her she had to ask me first. Now she can no longer get around me the way she used to. It was as if I had no authority as head of my household. And now Bob and I feel even closer to each other."

Even when a mother-in-law is not manipulative or vying for the attention of her son, the son must recognize the inherent tensions of the relationship between mother-in-law and daughter-in-law. Because a wife cannot tell her husband's mother, for example, "to stop complaining and cooperate" without causing damage to her marriage and their relationship, the husband must assume responsibility for assertive communications involving aspects of his mother's care.

If the parent-in-law is seriously disabled and requires hands-on personal care, support from the husband/son is critical. As we mentioned earlier, daughters-in-law rendering this care experience more negative stress effects than any other category of relative.[4] Although sons cannot be expected to give personal care to their mothers—nor do most mothers expect or want this from sons—they can be helpful in a variety of ways. Doing the laundry, changing the linens, marketing and shopping, preparing and cooking food, and transportation to doctors' appointments are important caregiving chores that lighten the load on their caregiving wives. A real partnership where gender does not determine who does what makes a dramatic difference in marital satisfaction and the wife's physical and emotional well-being.

On an emotional level, husbands can provide much needed support. They can affirm to their wives that it is okay for them to feel anger or resentment. They can listen when their wives voice how exhausted and frustrated they are. Women, socialized to be nurturers, to take care and to please others, have a hard time calling attention to their distress without feeling deep guilt. The special sensibilities of women in terms of internalized imperatives to rescue, to please, to make others happy, beg understanding by husbands in the context of the shared household. Believing they are not doing "their job" or not doing enough, many women in pushing themselves to do more, ultimately burn out and fall ill. Support and application of necessary perspective from an intelligently concerned husband can make a difference.

Husbands incapable of giving their wives emotional support must encourage their wives to join support groups or seek counseling. Better yet, as a couple, they might consider getting help. Caregiving daughters in general, but specifically daughters-in-law in shared households, must have an outlet for expressing their feelings. Venting their anger, resentment, and frustration in a safe environment with a professional or with peers is one of the best antidotes to burnout. The acknowledgment by husbands of their wives' sacrifices and hard work to give their mothers quality care is perhaps the most valuable gift of all. After all, when a daughter-in-law cares for her husband's mother, she has shown her love for him and a commitment to their marriage that he would be hard put to equal.

From Our Home to Nursing Home

Identification of Issues If Nursing Home Placement Becomes a Reality

The hardest decision adult daughters and sons have to make in the process of caring for their elderly parents is when to place a parent in a nursing home. Even when all other options to keep a parent home have been exhausted, the adult child still feels she has somehow failed in discharging her filial responsibilities. Even when the decision to place is made through mutual negotiation between parent and child leading to the former's consent, that parent may still feel abandoned. Even under the best of circumstances no one feels good about such a decision. Sadness and grief are the rule for both parent and child for some time to come. For many adult children, the grief experienced after a parent dies pales in contrast to the despair evoked by nursing home placement. It is, without question, the most painful of all the decisions concerning long-term care.

Although nursing home placement does not have the finality of death, both parent and child know it represents a parent's last move. One parent told the authors: "I view nursing home as the living cemetery to preceed the one where everyone is dead." An adult child in a similar vein intoned: "When I placed my mother in a nursing home, I felt as if I had placed her live on a funeral pyre. I also wondered whether I would ever be able to enjoy life again." Furthermore, nursing home visits do nothing to relieve this guilt, but rather act as a constant reminder to the child of what she has done. If a parent has difficulty adjusting, and many do as part of the natural process of grieving over loss of life as they once knew it, the child's guilt is even greater.

What one hears when listening to these adult children is their overwhelming sense of having committed a terrible crime, of having—in a manner of speaking—killed their parents. Even when all evidence indicates that placement is the only recourse, they continue to feel they have reneged on their filial responsibilities. Lack of family support, especially from siblings, and society's negative attitudes about placement exacerbate preexisting feelings of shame, guilt, and failure. Is it any wonder then that after placement, adult children find they are depressed, anxious, irritable, prone to crying spells, and unable to sleep or concentrate? A memorable statement from an adult child epitomizes the despair: "I am always thinking of my mother and what is happening to her there. Are they taking good care of her? I used to feed her myself to make sure she would eat enough and walk her with her walker to make sure she would have necessary exercise. I'm afraid they're not doing these things as well as I did or perhaps not at all. I know they're not spending the same amount of time with her. I just know she's alone and depressed all day. And I always kept her in clean clothes. How can I be sure they are doing the same in the nursing home? I know that when she has to use the bathroom, they are never on time. Once I found her soiled. I'm always thinking about my mother, all day, even on the job. I keep thinking there's something I could have done to keep this awful thing from happening to her. I feel because of me she has lost her dignity and reason to go on living. All day I feel guilty or angry and sometimes I know I'm very depressed because I cry a lot. I keep thinking there was something I could have done to keep her home. I feel I have betrayed her and myself in some deep, deep way."

Oddly enough, the feelings suffered by adult children of having deliberately abandoned their parents are often exacerbated by the active but appropriate role they must take in disposing of a parent's personal possessions after placement. Feeling they have no right to invade a parent's personal domain while a parent is still alive, many report a deep sense of guilt. They feel that they are somehow "betraying" their parents. Were the parent dead, the task would surely feel proper. An adult child told one of us that while going through her mother's drawers, closets, and storage boxes, she wanted to call her in the nursing home to ask her to make the final decision about what to keep or discard. Some adult children, additionally, relate that the necessary role they play in researching and selecting the best nursing home intensifies rather than diminishes guilt. To them, it does not feel like planning but like premeditation. It would seem that even when the child does what is right, she is in a no-win situation. Such are the feelings—conflict, frustration, shame, guilt—that overwhelm adult children as they struggle with their consciences in making the decision to place a parent.

Although most parents in shared households do not finish their final years in a nursing home, parents and children who live together experience special problems when placement becomes necessary. When a parent has been a flesh-and-blood presence in her child's home and an integral part of daily family life and the decision to place is made, abandonment of a parent is more than an abstraction. Some children feel they are literally "giving" a parent away or "throwing" her out the door. Feeling they are "bad" children who failed their parents by not finding some way to keep them in their home, they are pounded with unrelenting guilt and shame. Unlike parents and children who live separately, the adult child, after placement continues to be haunted by familiar ghosts: mother napping in her favorite chair; mother folding laundry at the kitchen table; mother watching the news with her. A cold emptiness exists where once there was human warmth.

For the daughter who has ministered the most personal, delicate hands-on care to her mother on a daily basis and can read her every wish by the look in her eyes, the thought of strangers doing those same things is painful and intolerable. She correctly knows no one will be able to care for Mother as lovingly as she or so completely understand her needs. Indeed, with each nursing home visit to validate her convictions, she would like to whisk Mother back to her home. Never mind that she can no longer has the strength herself to perform heavy personal chores or that the skilled assistance Mother now requires can only be given in a nursing home! She feels she can do and give better.

When a mother and daughter are close and taking care of Mom is a source of gratification, a daughter may postpone placement to her own and her parent's detriment. Some children hold off placement until the onset of dementia, hoping the parent's unawareness will ease their pain. The difficulty with this strategy is that neither the onset nor duration of severe dementia is predictable and by the time a parent is mentally nonfunctional, the caregiver herself may be close to collapse from the burden of caregiving.

A sixty-two-year-old daughter who had been caring for her mother in her home for five years and hoped to delay placement until her mother was totally disoriented relates the following: "The trouble was that her body went faster than her mind. Even though she no longer knew my name and talked gibberish, she could still give me a warm smile or squeeze my hand—enough recognition to give me a pang of guilt and harden my resolve to continue caring for her in my home. She was a lovely woman, always good to me, and I did not want to put her in a nursing home until she was absolutely out of it. But the physical work was killing me, and I wasn't sleeping nights because she was up a lot. She was so sweet, really, with the disposition of a saint. My husband and I though realized we couldn't go on this way; we were destroying *our* lives. So we found a home for her nearby and the staff didn't mind if I came over a lot to help. Although I miss her beyond anything I can express, I feel much better. I now know I should have placed her sooner and not waited."

The factor determining placement for Norma, sixty-six, who cared for her husband's mother for three years was her own depression. Having enjoyed a close relationship with her mother-in-law, Norma felt she could no longer bear to witness her transformation from a once-vibrant, competent woman into a shell. Although the hands-on personal care Norma ministered was exhausting, Norma felt her own depression and sadness pushed her into considering placement. "I think I could have cared for her until she died, were it not for my own emotional torment over her deterioration. I found myself crying all the time, not sleeping well, and nothing, but nothing could make me happy, including the laughter of my grandchildren. I knew she could no longer live with us, or I would be destroyed."

Because of the unique physical and psychological closeness between parent and child in the shared household, a child's judgment of what is in the best interests of her parent, herself, and her family can be skewed. Denial, set in motion by the infinite rewards of giving care to a loving and loved parent, is a potent force. Concrete and affectional tasks like cooking a parent's favorite dish or making her comfortable with an extra pillow or being there at the right time to give a hug are invested with the finest of human emotions. What better way to say "thank you for all that you've given me." For the adult child to know that she can make a positive difference in her parent's limited life brings a deep feeling of accomplishment and enhanced self-worth.

The darker side is that sooner or later the caregiver's needs obscure the parent's needs, preventing her from acknowledging the necessity of making a change. On a level that is not conscious, the child's need to be needed, in other words, the secondary gains she derives from the process of giving care take on a life of their own and become a kind of raison d'être for the caregiver herself. Simultaneously running a household, holding a job, taking care of a parent, and being a spouse give some caregivers a sense of mastery never before experienced. With a zeal bordering on compulsion or even addiction, the adult child cannot surrender control to others although this may be precisely what is called for at a particular time. For the caregiver to admit that perhaps she is now taking care of a parent for her own sake rather than for the parent's demands courage and honesty. It is, furthermore, not a simple matter to determine when caregiving genuinely expresses love and a desire to care or when under the compelling guise of love and care it is in reality self-serving. It is always hard to let go of those things that make us feel good about ourselves. Caregiving can be one of those things, more powerful and invidious than other tasks because of its inherent message that to care is to be good.

An adult daughter, Donna, fifty-eight, married, with a full-time job teaching elementary school, shared a household with her mother for almost seven years. When Donna finally agreed to place her mother in a nursing home, her mother was incontinent and unable to walk or care for herself. By then Donna's marriage was severely strained, and Donna herself was in poor health. Suffering from colitis, hypertension, and chronic backache from lifting, she was physically and emotionally exhausted. An only child whose relationship with her mother was close and loving and for whom "taking care" symbolized all the wonderful things her mother meant to her, Donna could only consider placement when crisis endangered her life.

For almost two years before placement, Donna's schedule classified as a model of industry and efficiency. Rising before six to take Mother to the commode and to do laundry and prepare meals, and staying up until twelve to give Mother her final medication, she arrived in her classroom all smiles, but churning inside. Often, as well, she would peek in during her lunch hour to check on the aide or, weather permitting, take Mother for a walk in her wheelchair. With two hospitalizations (the first time for a stroke and the second time for congestive heart failure and renal failure) in the two years that preceded placement, Mother clearly required round-the-clock, skilled care. Although Donna was advised of this necessity each time Mother was discharged from the hospital, she insisted upon bringing her home. She later told one of us:

> I could not let her go. She had become such a big part of my life. It was as if my life depended upon her staying with me, not the other way around. When my husband and children became angry with me for neglecting my health and them, I became furious and denied that taking care of Mother was having ill effects upon me. I didn't see how I could stop caring for her. Actually I was pleased that I could manage all my responsibilities so well. At times I was on a real "high." Eventually, I sought help from a psychotherapist who helped me to see how psychologically entangled I was with my mother. In a sense, I didn't know where she began and I left off. My needs had become hers.

At the time of this interview, Donna's mother had been in a nursing home for six months. She was adjusting well; in fact, much better than Donna, for whom life now seemed empty.

Living with rather than apart from a parent also has a strange way of blurring the physical changes that time writes on aging faces and bodies. The child who sees her parent every few weeks or months is often in a better position to observe physical or mental decline. Not having seen Mother in three months, a visiting sibling, for example, cannot believe how much more frail she has become or how much more slowly she moves her feet. The primary caregiver, on the other hand, with whom Mom lives, is oblivious to the changes. As with married couples, young parents and children, or anyone, in fact, who lives with another person, proximity has a peculiar way of filtering out the inevitable wear and tear wrought by time.

Changes in parental functioning seem to come silently, invisibly, when parent and child live together. One daughter summed it up thus:

> One day I saw it was taking me almost two hours to get Mom ready for her adult day care program. When I finished bathing and dressing her, I was completely exhausted. By the time I regained my energy and strength, it was time for her to return home and I had to reverse the process. I could not believe she needed so much help. I could not believe she had changed so much; nor could I bear to believe it. It was too painful for me to see my once active and capable mother so needy. Mom had been living with me for four years. In the beginning she required so little and was even a help with household chores. I don't understand. These changes were taking place in front of my very eyes. I guess I was too close to see them.

Because all the forces defining closeness—nurturance love, protection, care, and comfort—are intensified when parent and child live together, the reality of separation is harder to assimilate. In essence, the dynamics of togetherness and separation confront the caregiver who lives with a parent in a different and more powerful manner than her counterpart who cares for a parent from afar. Not only does the togetherness—the close physical and psychological connection—magnify the impact of the inevitable separation and loss but it makes the initiation of discussing necessary long-terms plans extremely painful. The majority of our respondents from shared households had *not* discussed placement in a nursing home with their parents. The following is typical of their reasoning: "I couldn't put her in one of those places; that's why she is with us. My mother and I never talk about it, because she knows I will never do that to her; she would die if she ever had to leave our home for one of those places. It's absolutely out of the question and has always been right from the beginning; she wouldn't do it to me if the situation were reversed—why should I do it to her?"

Yet, these caregivers were unable to put the subject to rest. All felt anxiety and fear that mounted in intensity with passing months and years. Though never mentioned, the dreaded subject of placement continued to hover like a dark cloud over and between their parents and them, creating distance rather than intimacy.

The possibility of nursing home placement must be discussed by parent and child before they move in with each other. In fact, it should be part of the living-together agreement. Witholding discussion until after the parent settles in usually backfires. As with all uncomfortable subject matter, avoiding it only heightens the dread of eventual confrontation. Openly discussed as one of the many options of long-term care *before* a parent moves in and while that parent is independent, nursing home placement loses some of its power to frighten. Additionally, broaching the subject early on affords the parent control over her life by giving her time to digest its full meaning. When placement does become necessary, it will not be a surprise. She will know that she is not being abruptly "dumped." With the additional reassurance from her children that placement does not mean emotional abandonment, she will feel secure in the knowledge that although her address may change, her child's love and commitment to her remain.

The story of Miriam, Aaron, and Aaron's mother, Mary, begun in Chapter 5, poignantly illustrates how nursing home placement was managed by a particular family. This story is well worth examining as an example to all parents and children who live together lovingly.

Mary, who had lived with her son, Aaron, and daughter-in-law, Miriam, for twelve years without mishap suddenly fell and broke her hip. Following surgery and rehabilitation, Mary came home to her family, with all hoping she could remain there indefinitely. Miriam and Aaron immediately obtained a nurse for Mary. Mary learned to use a walker and initially did quite well. Within a few months, however, she became confused about her medications and came to need supervision. Mary's bedroom was next to Miriam and Aaron's so that they were able to hear her when she needed assistance. In time, however, Mary's confusion increased. She required more care than her children could provide. Many times she awoke during the night confused and disoriented and would call Miriam for help. Because of these frequent nocturnal interruptions, Miriam was unable to get sufficient sleep and found it difficult to function at her teaching job.

Loving Mary very much, Miriam and Aaron would have kept her home had Medicaid paid for home health care seven days a week, eight hours a day, instead of five days at four hours each day. Consequently, when they were forced to consider placement in a nursing home for Mary, they did so sadly and reluctantly. Miriam, who still suffered from the guilt of placing her own mother several years earlier, told us: "I absolutely hated putting her there; it was reliving the nightmare all over again."

Although Miriam and Aaron told Mary what they felt they had to do and she seemed to understand, Mary was initially very unhappy in her new home. Whenever Miriam and Aaron visited, she asked when they were going to take her home. After a while, however, she seemed to settle in and she stopped asking to leave. Since Aaron was retired by the time Mary was placed, he was able to visit his mother every day. Miriam visited several times a week, and grandchildren who lived nearby came as often as they could, usually bringing their children, Mary's great grandchildren with them. They were a close family, willing and able to give Mary sufficient love and affection so that she never felt emotionally abandoned by those who mattered to her.

Unlike Mary, who had lived with her children a long time, Joyce's mother, Doris, moved in following a brief hospitalization for surgery. Believing Doris would only be a temporary guest, returning shortly to her own apartment, Joyce did not think to discuss other living options with her mother. Eight months later, with Mother's recovery proceeding sporadically and slowly, Joyce found herself in a real dilemma. With an angry husband on her hands, a canceled vacation, and other disruptions in lifestyle, Joyce felt trapped into caring for her mother. She could not bring herself to broach the subject of placement, now necessary because Joyce herself was becoming exhausted from providing more care than she could realistically give.

In the course of recovery of a frail, aged person, weeks easily turn into months; a short stay becomes a lengthy one; family life is stressed by disruptions in routine and style. Long-term plans must be discussed by both parties before any move to live together is made.

Although the nursing home population in this country is actually quite low (approximately 5 percent of those over sixty-five are in nursing homes), the extensive coverage of substandard nursing homes by the media gives the impression that the majority of the elderly end their days in one of these facilities. As Brody points out, those currently in nursing homes represent a fairly exclusive grouping. Nursing home residents, by and large, are severely disabled, well into old age (average age 81), female, and single.[1] Most elderly in this country manage to live out their days in the community, with more living independently than ever before.

Certainly many nursing homes deserve criticism. Some are indeed horrible places. And it is no wonder that adult children shudder at the thought of placing a parent in one. Others, however, do an exemplary job of caring for our parents and grandparents. Alive with the comforting sounds of conversation and the hubbub of stimulating activities, they are truly "homes" where people have come to live rather than to die. Staff are friendly and pleasant; residents, whether in wheelchairs or ambulatory, are not isolated in their rooms but mingle with aides, visitors, and volunteers in lounges and common areas. One senses that such places are more than institutions; here is where people are cared about and for; where that oft-touted word, "dignity," is given real meaning.

These "good" nursing homes can be identified. Nursing home inspection reports are no longer secret but open to the public. State departments of health are required to release nursing home deficiency profiles to whoever wishes this information. State divisions of Medicaid provide vast amounts of educational material to consumers, outlining what to look for and what questions to ask in choosing a home. Both parent and child, therefore, can have significant control over the selection process.

Once a parent is in the home, the adult child can continue to play an active part in her parent's life, including taking a parent out for visits, meals, entertainment, family parties, and so forth. If a parent cannot be taken out but is mentally intact, she still wants to be part of her children's life. Parents, whether in homes or institutions, want to feel and know they are still needed by their children; they want that vital connection with family—that sense of belonging. Having not surrendered their passion for lively conversation to infirmity, they crave news (both good and bad) and gossip about relatives and family happenings. If anything, because of increased physical and social limitations imposed by their new environment, they are more eager than ever to provide advice or snippets of wisdom. As children demonstrate to their parents that they value them for who they are and what they know, they enable their parents to ascend to that most honorable and meaningful role of sage or mentor, more fully explained in Chapter 5. Without the pressure of caregiving chores, the visiting child now has the energy for close, genuine encounters. Indeed, freed of the negative emotions of resentment and guilt, she may for the first time be open to really getting to know her parent as a person. Encouraging a parent to talk about the past (see Chapter 8 for the discussion of "reminiscence"), the adult child affirms to her parent that she and her life matter; that the lessons she shares will not only be remembered by children but retold to grandchildren and grandchildren's children. One need not dedicate a library wing or donate a work of art to a museum to insure the immortality of a beloved parent. Transmission of wisdom to succeeding generations is an equally meaningful way for a parent to participate in ongoing life.

Children can and do make a critical difference in the life of their parents in nursing homes. By bringing the outside world in, they not only expand the walls of their parent's new home but continue to give them that vital sense of connection to family. Giving care to a parent does not end with placement. The physical and concrete caregiving chores cease; the emotional care—the more valuable of the two sides to caregiving— endures.

Even parents suffering from dementia, who no longer know who and where they are respond to the stuff of emotional caregiving. A hug, caress, or squeeze of the hand bring a kind of awakening. Confusion does not blunt a parent's ability to feel. Children who bear this special pain, therefore, can still bring meaning to their nursing home visits with nonverbal communication.

The adult child must understand that the first six months of nursing home placement are the most difficult and crucial. Until a parent settles in, and some, sadly, do not, the child will not only witness her parent's grief over the inexorable loss of her home, but struggle with her own feelings attendant to her parent's adjustment. Adjustment is an individual matter, determined by a parent's capacity to adapt to change and ability to form social connections. Those who adjust experience greater levels of life satisfaction in the nursing home than living at home.[2] With social stimulation provided by interaction with peers and staff and a diminution of feelings of inadequacy resulting from living with others who are similarly impaired, parents may actually feel better about themselves. Current research cites that parents living with persons who are healthy and active may experience less self-esteem.

An important resource to utilize during this six-month period is the social service staff of the nursing home. Children should not hesitate to talk to these professionals about whatever aspects of nursing home care they do not understand or find troublesome. Social workers, moreover, will be happy to differentiate what is normal adjustment behavior from what is not. They will offer suggestions on how to help your parent through this transition. Many nursing home social workers run support or discussion groups for adult children to aid them through this period of adjustment and to teach them the ins and outs of the nursing home system so they can advocate for their parent effectively. If these groups exist, children will find them extremely helpful. If they do not, suggest to the social worker that she form them. Children can even be instrumental in developing these groups by offering to assist with phone calls and other administrative chores. Children can go a step further and actually become nursing home volunteers. By bridging the gap between what adult children can actually do now that the parent is no longer with them and what they feel they should do, such involvement diminishes feelings of helplessness and guilt.

Middle-aged caregivers must understand that the expression "quality care" extends to the caregiver and her family as well as to the parent to whom the care is given. The internalized moral imperative to return total care and the misinterpretation of role reversal to mean that parents become babies to be cared for by their children reinforce unrealistic expectations in the caregiver. Taking a parent to the commode, helping a parent into the bathtub, turning a parent to prevent bed sores, changing the soiled protective wear of an incontinent parent are not comparable to the chores of child rearing. Such laborious care exacts great personal toll on the caregiver and her family and is better done in a skilled care facility. The middle-aged daughter who cares for her mother bears little resemblance to her younger, more energetic counterpart and needs all the help she can get. Placement of a parent in a nursing home when appropriate, carries with it neither shame nor disgrace.

In discussing nursing home placement with a parent early, the parent truly becomes a partner in the entire decision-making process.[3] Allowing the parent time to think about and digest the meaning of such a move gives her control over her destiny. Recent studies clearly point out that when parents are prepared by their children or significant others for placement, their anxiety is considerably diminished.[4] Of course, when and if placement becomes a reality, the parent, if at all possible, must play an active role in selecting the home in which she wishes to live.

Nursing home placement may be one of many steps in the process of giving long-term care to an elderly parent. It has its time and place, determined by the physical and medical needs of the parent and by the physical, emotional, family, and often medical needs of the caregiver.

For those considering nursing home placement for a parent, the authors recommend Nancy Fox's *You, Your Parent and the Nursing Home* (see Selected Readings in appendix B) as a helpful resource. It is concise and sensitively written, yet filled with essential guidelines for the adult child caregiver.

Future Possibilities

Caregiving, Eldercare, Co-Housing

As the twenty-first century approaches, two things are certain: (1) the number of old people in this country will increase; and (2) families, though shrinking in size, will continue to give the bulk of care to their elderly parents. With the segment of the population over eighty-five predicted to grow from 3.3 million to 13 million over the next fifty years,[1] parents, though living longer, will be living more functionally impaired lives. Consequently, the chronic illnesses of advanced old age that reduce the ability of the elderly to live independently will insure the permanence of the shared household as a realistic option. Although the percentage of elderly women living in a shared household has decreased from 45 percent in 1950 to 25 percent in 1977, families, nevertheless, will continue to choose this arrangement for the same economic, social, and medical reasons outlined in the Introduction.[2]

The bond between the elderly parent and the adult child is strong, and evidence indicates that it will remain so. From our work with hundreds of families, we are convinced that the next generation is as committed to caring for their parents as this one. Indeed, as the world becomes ever more depersonalized, human relationships assume even greater importance. The commandment to honor thy father and mother is alive and well; adult children continue to assume their filial responsibilities. As Elaine Brody aptly notes: "The notion that family values about care of the aged have weakened and that the formal system provides most of the helping services is another expression of the myth of isolation and abandonment. The family, not professionals and the bureaucracy, is the main source of assistance to disabled elderly."[3]

As the birth rate continues to decline and as women continue to enter the work force, there are fewer and fewer adult children and fewer and fewer daughters staying home. Parents who live with their children will find themselves spending large blocks of time alone without healthy outlets for friendship and socialization.

More and more women are single parents or "remarrieds" with new "blended" families. This change in the lifestyles of women further complicates the future of elder care. That some caregivers themselves will be over sixty-five when called upon to give care to their parents adds yet another feature to the landscape of caregiving in the next century. With so many changes in family forms and relationships, private and public sectors of our nation will be pressed to find innovative ways to care compassionately and comprehensively for an aging population whose adult children are overwhelmed with multiple pressures and responsibilities. Improvement in the delivery of support services, increased housing assistance with changes in zoning codes, and eldercare for working children are some of the necessary directions to pursue.

Already, companies such as Stride Rite in Massachusetts offer intergenerational centers for employees' children *and* elderly dependents. Such programs enable working daughters, otherwise anxious about their homebound parents, to bring them to work. With Mother on the premises, Daughter need not make check-up phone calls during the work day; her morale is surely better. IBM is also in step with the future with its Elder Care Referral Service, whose stated goal is "to help with the often complex and sometimes stressful responsibility of caring for aging relatives." Free to all employees, caregivers pay only for the services their parents receive. With dramatic increases in absenteeism, tardiness, and time away from the job caused by the demands of elder care, these programs not only make sense but in the long run save money.[4]

With parents living longer than ever and more daughters working, a future possibility is the increased use of flextime for employed caregivers, especially those who are caring for parents in their own homes. Part-time jobs with full benefits and job-sharing options may also become part of the workplace scene. With 12 percent of women currently leaving their jobs to care for an elderly parent, labor unions, management, and government must explore new ways to enable women to work and care for their parents in the next century.[5]

In a study conducted by the New York City Office on Aging, it was found that company eldercare services, where available, were used not only by active caregivers but also by employees who anticipated becoming caregivers in the future (validating the commitment of the next generation to care for their parents). The study concluded: "The use of an eldercare service by pre-caregivers supports the concept of a preventive approach in assisting caregivers by making information available in the workplace that may avert or ameliorate difficulties and crises when caregiving becomes a reality and, thus, have a more severe impact on worker's job performance."[6]

Because many interpersonal problems in the shared household are caused by lack of privacy and space, the importance of finding some way to give a parent the basics of private room and bath cannot be overstated. A private apartment within the child's home or an attached wing provide generations with necessary havens where they can enjoy some solitude. ECHO housing, mentioned in Chapter 7, might prove to be the best solution to this problem. With a separate cottage adjacent to the adult child's home, the elderly parent can live near her children without living with them. She can enjoy the security of having family nearby and the independence of coming and going as she pleases. Although zoning codes and public attitudes have severely limited the use of ECHO housing in this country, statistics show that ECHO cottages are now being seen in a more favorable light. According to Ken Dychtwald, "Thirteen percent of all prefabricated manufactured houses are currently located not in mobile home parks but upon the property of families and friends."[7] Furthermore, ECHO housing, while offering the same benefits —economy, independence, support, security, and companionship—as house sharing, goes a step further in that it affords parents more privacy and control than any other "living together" arrangement.

Although home equity conversion loans are one source of financing home modifications for elderly parents, the need exists for additional government programs. Subsidies, low interest loans, and loan guarantees are options for the future.

We hope that opposition to housing options such as ECHO and accessory apartments will continue to fade as the number of elderly people increases and the costs of housing and nursing home care soar. The American Association of Retired Persons (AARP) has already mounted a campaign to educate the public about the benefits of ECHO housing. Communities faced with shortages of affordable housing may come to realize that permitting accessory apartments, for example, is an excellent way to make productive use of unused space in many homes, while extending a lifeline to elderly parents who wish to live with their children.

One also hopes that the future will bring an end to onerous zoning restrictions that regulate the composition of households. Regulating land use as a legitimate concern of municipalities is justified; restricting living arrangements within households to a narrow, traditional definition of family is an invasion of basic rights. Although some states have ruled against these restrictions, they have been upheld in others.

Co-housing living arrangements, begun in Denmark, and already in wide use in Holland, Sweden, Germany, and France, may make their appearance on the American housing scene in the twenty-first century. Designed for people of all ages, not just the elderly, they permit a wide diversity of homeowners. Encompassing married couples, singles, single parents, couples with and without children, they reflect the world as it is and will create a richer community than one where the "old" are isolated from the rest of society. Co-housing allows each family unit a private dwelling complete with kitchen, but also provides communal facilities such as dining rooms, workshops, guestrooms, children's playrooms, and laundry facilities. It has been said of co-housing that "it fills the gap between shared housing and single-family houses, combining the advantages of an intergenerational community with the autonomy of private units."[8] Although there are a few examples of some aspects of this type of planned community in the United States, it is basically in its infancy here. Because it offers not only an excellent housing option for older parents and their middle-aged children, but also a better place for families to raise children and for older adults to socialize with people of all ages, it may become the wave of the future.

As our aging population grows and more people require long-term care, respite care services will become even more crucial as a source of support for beleaguered caregivers. For parents and children who live together, their value is immeasurable. Both out-of-house and in-house respite services should increase in coming years. Currently, public funding for out-of-house respite services is minimal, with only a few pilot projects operating in key areas.

At the time of this writing, however, Senator Bill Bradley of New Jersey has introduced the Family Caregiver Support Act of 1991. Contained in this bill are provisions for an array of necessary respite care services for primary caregivers of functionally impaired persons, to include companion services, personal assistance, homemaker services, home health services, adult day care, temporary care in licensed or accredited facilities, and peer support and training. "Services may be provided on an hourly, daily, or overnight basis, according to an individual service plan based on an assessment of the caregiver and care recipient's particular needs."[9] Because eligibility requirements for services are broader than in existing programs, more middle-class families will be able to qualify for assistance.

The private sector, composed of religious and civic organizations, does its share as well. Interfaith Caregivers, Inc., of Moorestown, New Jersey, is a stellar example of what private citizens can do. Begun in 1983 by nine churches in the Moorestown area and spearheaded by Dr. Fred Missel, a retired minister, Interfaith Caregivers now has over two hundred trained volunteers in its program and has spawned two other groups. The supportive in-house services provided include help with light meals and filling out forms, reading, shopping, telephone reassurance, and transportation. Volunteers are trained by professionals but their services are free of charge. Today, Interfaith Caregivers is recognized as an indispensible source of supportive home care services by social service agencies, hospitals, and area offices on aging. Such groups perform significant services and they will surely increase over the coming years.

The future will in all likelihood see a proliferation in the number of people—retired and younger—who for a moderate fee are willing to perform a variety of necessary chores and services for the elderly. Shopping, food marketing, writing checks, doing household repair jobs, and filling out health insurance forms are included in the array of tasks these persons can do. For many, the aging of America will provide opportunities to do well while doing good.

Because the need for services will increase and the existence of supportive services does not guarantee their use, the years ahead will witness increased communication efforts to give people necessary information on the "wheres" and "hows" of the formal (government and social agencies) support system. Radio and television programs and community seminars sponsored by state and area offices on aging, local colleges, and civic and religious organizations will educate consumers about community and other supportive caregiving services. Lectures, seminars, and town meetings will address the problems of eldercare; flyers, leaflets, and information brochures will be available in shops and markets as well as local government offices; small shopping newspapers and supermarket bulletin boards will be filled with names of people and groups who are willing to come to the rescue of stressed caregivers.

If the years to come bring peace, future possibilities for the improvement of eldercare in this country abound. With recognition by private and public sectors that the crisis in caregiving is not just the family's problem but society's, those who ask, "Should Mom live with us?" will know that whatever their answer, help and hope are out there.

Appendix A

State Units on Aging

Alabama

Commission on Aging
136 Catoma Street, Second Floor
Montgomery, AL 36130
(205) 242-5743

Alaska

Older Alaskans Commission
Department of Administration
Pouch C—Mail Station 0209
Juneau, AK 99811
(907) 465-3250

Arizona

Aging and Adult Administration
Department of Economic Security
1400 West Washington Street
Phoenix, AZ 85007
(602) 542-4446

Arkansas

Division of Aging and Adult Services
Arkansas Department of Human Services
P.O. Box 1417, SLOT 1412
Seventh and Main Streets
Little Rock, AR 72201
(501) 682–2441

California

Department of Aging
1600 K Street
Sacramento, CA 95814
(916) 322–5290

Colorado

Aging and Adult Service
Department of Social Services
1575 Sherman Street, Tenth Floor
Denver, CO 80203
(303) 866–3851

Connecticut

Department on Aging
175 Main Street
Hartford, CT 06106
(203) 566–3238

Delaware

Division on Aging
Department of Health and Social Services
1901 North DuPont Highway
New Castle, DE 19720
(302) 421–6791

District of Columbia

Office on Aging
1424 K Street N.W.
Second Floor
Washington, D.C. 20005
(202) 724–5626

Florida

Program Office of Aging and Adult Services
Department of Health and Rehabilitative Services
1317 Winewood Boulevard
Tallahassee, FL 32301
(904) 488–8922

Georgia

Office of Aging
878 Peachtree Street, N.E.
Room 632
Atlanta, GA 30309
(404) 894–5333

Guam

Division of Senior Citizens
Department of Public Health & Social Services
Government of Guam
Post Office Box 2816
Agana, Guam 96910

Hawaii

Executive Office on Aging
Office of the Governor
335 Merchant Street
Room 241
Honolulu, HI 96813
(808) 548–2593

Idaho

Office on Aging
Room 108—Statehouse
Boise, ID 83720
(208) 334–3833

Illinois

Department on Aging
421 East Capitol Avenue
Springfield, IL 62701
(217) 785–2870

Indiana

Choice/Home Care Services
Department of Human Services
251 North Illinois Street
P.O. Box 7083
Indianapolis, IN 46207
(317) 232–7020

Iowa

Department of Elder Affairs
Suite 236, Jewett Building
914 Grand Avenue
Des Moines, IA 50319
(515) 281–5187

Kansas

Department on Aging
Docking State Office Building, 122-S
915 S.W. Harrison
Topeka, KS 66612
(913) 296–4986

Kentucky

Division of Aging Services
Cabinet for Human Resources
CHR Building—Sixth West
275 East Main Street
Frankfort, KY 40621
(502) 564–6930

Louisiana

Office of Elderly Affairs
4550 N. Boulevard—Second Floor
P.O. Box 80374
Baton Rouge, LA 70806
(504) 925–1700

Maine

Bureau of Elder & Adult Services
Department of Human Services
State House—Station #11
Augusta, ME 04333
(207) 626–5335

Maryland

Office on Aging
State Office Building
301 West Preston Street—Room #1004
Baltimore, MD 21201
(301) 225-1100

Massachusetts

Executive Office of Elder Affairs
38 Chauncy Street
Boston, MA 02111
(617) 727-7750

Michigan

Office of Services to the Aging
P.O. Box 30026
Lansing, MI 48909
(517) 373-8230

Minnesota

Board on Aging
444 Lafayette Road
St. Paul, MN 55155
(612) 296-2770

Mississippi

Council on Aging
Division of Aging and Adult Services
421 West Pascagoula Street
Jackson, MS 39203
(601) 949-2070

Missouri

Division on Aging
Department of Social Services
P.O. Box 1337—615 Howerton Court
Jefferson City, MO 65102
(314) 751–3082

Montana

The Governor's Office on Aging
State Capitol Building
Capitol Station, Room 219
Helena, MT 59620
(406) 444–3111

Nebraska

Department on Aging
P.O. Box 95044
301 Centennial Mall—South
Lincoln, NE 68509
(402) 471–2306

Nevada

Division for Aging Services
Department of Human Resources
340 North Eleventh Street, Suite 114
Las Vegas, NV 89101
(702) 486–3545

New Hampshire

Division of Elderly & Adult Services
6 Hazen Drive
Concord, NH 03301
(603) 271–4680

New Jersey

Division on Aging
Department of Community Affairs
CN807
South Broad and Front Streets
Trenton, NJ 08625
(609) 292-4833

New Mexico

State Agency on Aging
224 East Palace Avenue—Fourth Floor
La Villa Rivera Building
Santa Fe, NM 87501
(505) 827-7640

New York

Office for the Aging
New York State Plaza
Agency Building -2
Albany, NY 12223
(518) 474-4425

North Carolina

Division of Aging
693 Palmer Drive
Raleigh, NC 27603
(919) 733-3983

North Dakota

Aging Services
Department of Human Services
State Capitol Building
Bismark, ND 58505
(701) 224-2577

Northern Mariana Islands

Office of Aging
Department of Community and Cultural Affairs
Civic Center—Susupe
Saipan, Northern Mariana Islands 96950
Telephone: 9411 or 9732

Ohio

Department of Aging
50 West Broad Street—Ninth Floor
Columbus, OH 43266
(614) 455–5500

Oklahoma

Aging Services Division
Department of Human Services
P.O. Box 25352
Oklahoma City, OK 73125
(405) 521–2327

Oregon

Senior and Disabled Services Division
313 Public Service Building
Salem, OR 97310
(503) 378–4728

Pennsylvania

Department of Aging
231 State Street
Harrisburg, PA 17101
(717) 783–1550

Puerto Rico

Governor's Office for Elderly Affairs
Call Box 50063
Old San Juan Station
San Juan, PR 00902
(809) 721–5710

Rhode Island

Department of Elderly Affairs
160 Pine Street
Providence, RI 02903
(401) 277–2858

(American) Samoa

Territorial Administration on Aging
Office of the Governor
Pago Pago, American Samoa 96799
011 (684) 633–1252

South Carolina

Commission on Aging
Suite B-500
400 Arbor Lake Drive
Columbia, SC 29223
(803) 735–0210

South Dakota

Office of Adult Services and Aging
700 North Illinois Street
Kneip Building
Pierre, SD 57501
(605) 773–3656

Tennessee

Commission on Aging
Suite 201
706 Church Street
Nashville, TN 37243
(615) 741-2056

Texas

Department on Aging
P.O. Box 12786 Capitol Station
1949 IH 35, South
Austin, TX 78741
(512) 444-2727

Federated States of Micronesia

Federated States of Micronesia
Department of Human Resources
Kolonia, Pohnpei FM 96941
(691) 320-2733

Utah

Division of Aging and Adult Services
Department of Social Services
120 North—200 West
Box 45500
Salt Lake City, UT 84145
(801) 538-3910

Vermont

Aging and Disabilities
103 South Main Street
Waterbury, VT 05676
(802) 241-2400

Virginia

Department for the Aging
700 Centre, Tenth Floor
700 East Franklin Street
Richmond, VA 23219
(804) 225–2271

Virgin Islands

Senior Citizen Affairs
Department of Human Services
#19 Estate Diamond Fredericksted
St. Croix, VI 00840
(809) 772–4950 ext. 46

Washington

Aging and Adult Services Administration
Department of Social and Health Services
OB-44A
Olympia, WA 98504
(206) 586–3768

West Virginia

Commission on Aging
Holly Grove—State Capitol
Charleston, WV 25305
(304) 348–3317

Wisconsin

Bureau of Aging
Division of Community Services
217 South Hamilton Street Suite 300
Madison, WI 53707
(608) 266–2536

Wyoming

Commission on Aging
Hathaway Building—Room 139
Cheyenne, WY 82002
(307) 777-7986

Appendix B

General Resources

Organizations and Agencies

Action
806 Connecticut Avenue NW
Washington, DC 20525

Administration on Aging (AoA)
U.S. Department of Health and Human Services
330 Independence Avenue SW
Washington, DC 20201

Aging Network Services
Suite 907
4400 East-West Highway
Bethesda, MD 20814

American Association of Homes for the Aging (AAHA) and Continuing Care Accreditation Commission (CCAC)
1129 20 Street NW
Suite 400
Washington, DC 20036

American Association of Retired Persons (AARP)
1909 K Street NW
Washington, DC 20049

American Health Care Association
1201 L Street NW
Washington, DC 20005

Commission on Legal Problems of the Elderly
American Bar Association
1800 M Street NW
Washington, DC 20036

Consumer Information Center
P.O. Box 100
Pueblo, CO 81009

Consumer Product Safety Commission,
Office of Information & Public Affairs
5401 Westbard Avenue
Bethesda, MD 20207

Council of State Housing Agencies
400 N. Capitol Street NW
Suite 291
Washington, DC 20001

Elder Craftsmen
135 East 65 Street
New York, NY 10021

Elderhostel
Suite 400
80 Boylston Street
Boston, MA 02116

Farmers Home Administration (FmHA)
South Agriculture Building
14 Street & Independence Avenue SW
Washington, DC 20250

Gray Panthers
Suite 601
311 South Juniper Street
Philadelphia, PA 19107

Institute for Consumer Policy Research
256 Washington Street
Mt. Vernon, NY 10553

Life Safety Systems, Inc.
2100 M Street NW
#305
Washington, DC 20037

Manufactured Housing Institute, Public Affairs Dept.
1745 Jefferson Davis Highway
Arlington, VA 22202

Medic Alert Foundation
P.O. Box 1009
Turlock, CA 95381

National Action Forum for Midlife and Older Women
c/o Dr. Jane Porcino
P.O. Box 816
Stony Brook, NY 11790

National Alliance of Senior Citizens
2525 Wilson Boulevard
Arlington, VA 22201

National Association of Area Agencies on Aging (N4A)
1112 16 Street, NW
Suite 100
Washington, DC 20036

National Association of State Units on Aging
2033 K Street NW
Suite 304
Washington, DC 20006

National Association for Home Care
519 C Street NE
Washington, DC 20002

National Association of Housing and Redevelopment Officials
2600 Virginia Avenue
Washington, DC 20037

National Center for Home Equity Conversion
1210 East College Drive
Suite 300
Marshall, MN 56258

National Consumers League
1522 C Street NW
Suite 406
Washington, DC 20005

National Council of Senior Citizens
925 15 Street NW
Washington, DC 20005

National Council on the Aging (NCOA)
409 Third Street NW
Washington, DC 20024

National HomeCaring Council
235 Park Avenue South
New York, NY 10003

National Institute on Adult Day Care
Dept. P, 600 Maryland Avenue SW
West Wing 100
Washington, DC 20024

National Institute on Aging, Public Information Office
9000 Rockville Pike
Building 31, Room 5C35
Bethesda, MD 20892

National League for Nursing / American Public Health Association
10 Columbus Circle
New York, NY 10019

National Policy Center on Housing and Living Arrangements for Older Americans, University of Michigan
200 Bonistrel Boulevard
Ann Arbor, MI 48109

National Safety Council
444 North Michigan Avenue
Chicago, IL 60611

National Senior Citizens Law Center
Suite 400
2025 M Street NW
Washington, DC 20036

National Shared Housing Resource
6344 Greene Street
Philadelphia, PA 19144

Older Women's League (OWL)
Suite 300
730 11 Street NW
Washington, DC 20001

Share-A-Home Associates
701 Driver Avenue
Winter Park, FL 32789

American Association of Retired Persons (AARP)

AARP is an excellent resource for housing options and caregiving. To order copies of AARP materials, write to AARP Publications, Program Resources Department/BV, 1909 K Street NW, Washington, D.C. 20049. We recommend the following AARP publications for readers needing more information on the topics discussed in this book.

A Checklist of Concerns—Resources for Caregivers. Publication no. D12895.

CHISS: Consumer's Guide on Accessory Apartments. Publication no. D12775.

CHISS: Consumer's Guide to Home Sharing. Publication no. D12774.

CHISS: Local Housing Resources Guide. Publication no. D12785.

CHISS: Resource Guide on Accessory Apartments. Publication no. D12775.

CHISS: Resource Guide on Rental Housing. Publication no. D12773.

Congregate Housing. Publication no. D12141.

Continuing Care Retirement Communities. Publication no. D12181.

ECHO Housing Fact Sheet. Publication no. D1006.

A Handbook About Care in the Home. Publication no. D955.

A Home Away from Home: Consumer Information on Board and Care Homes. Publication no. D12446.

Housing Options for Older Americans. Publication no. D12063.

How to Protect Your Home. Publication no. D395.

Introducing CHISS (Consumer Housing Information Service for Seniors). Publication no. D12449.

Legal Issues: Accessory Apartments—Zoning Covenants Restricting Land to Residential Uses. Publication no. D1188.

Nursing Home Life: A Guide for Residents and Families. Publication no. D13063.

A Path for Caregivers. Publication no. D12957.

The Right Place at the Right Time—A Guide to Long-Term Care Choices. Publication no. D12381.

Selected Readings

American Association of Homes for the Aging. *Continuing Care Retirement Community: A Guidebook for Consumers.* Washington, D.C.: American Association of Homes for the Aging, 1983.

Bloomfield, Harold. *Making Peace With Your Parents.* New York: Ballantine Books, 1981.
Brody, Elaine M. *Women in the Middle: Their Parent Care Years.* New York: Springer, 1990.

Carlin, Vivian F., and Ruth Mansberg. *If I Live to Be 100: A Creative Housing Solution for Older People.* 2d ed. Princeton, N.J.: Princeton Book Co., 1989.
———. *Where Can Mom Live? A Family Guide to Living Arrangements for Older Parents.* Lexington, Mass.: Lexington Books, 1987.
Consumers' Guide to Home Adaptation. Boston: Adaptive Environments Center, June 1989. (A copy may be obtained for $1.00. Send request to 621 Huntington Avenue, Boston, MA 02115.)
Couper, Donna, P. *Aging and Our Families: Handbook for Family Caregivers.* New York: Human Science Press, 1989.

Dychtwald, Ken. *Age Wave.* New York: Bantam Books, 1990.

Edinberg, Mark A. *Talking with Your Aging Parents.* Boston: Shambhala, 1988.

Fox, Nancy. *You, Your Parent, and the Nursing Home.* Buffalo, N.Y.: Prometheus Books, 1988.

Greenberg, Vivian. *Your Best Is Good Enough: Aging Parents and Your Emotions.* Lexington, Mass.: Lexington Books, 1989.

Hancock, Judith Ann. *Housing for the Elderly.* New Brunswick, N.J.: Center for Urban Policy Research, 1987.
Hare, P. H. *Creating an Accessory Apartment.* New York: McGraw-Hill, 1986.
Home Care Assembly of New Jersey. *Home Health Care: A Consumer Guide.* Princeton, N.J.: Home Care Assembly of New Jersey, 1984.
Hooyman, N. R. *Taking Care: Supporting Older People and Their Families.* New York: Free Press, 1986.

Koch, Tom. *Mirrored Lives: Aging Children and Elderly Parents*. Westport, Conn.: Greenwood Publishing Group, 1990.

LaBuda, Dennis R., ed. *The Gadget Book: Ingenious Devices for Easier Living*. Glenview, Ill.: AARP, 1985.

National Association of Area Agencies on Aging. *Directory of State and Area Agencies on Aging and National Guide for Elder Care Information and Referral, 1989–90*. Washington, D.C.: National Association of Area Agencies on Aging, 1990.

National Council of Jewish Women, Aging Priority. *Options for Living Arrangements: Housing Alternatives for the Elderly*. 1980. (Available through National Council of Jewish Women, Aging Priority, 12 East 26 Street, New York, N.Y. 10010.)

National HomeCaring Council. *All About Home Care: A Consumers' Guide*. New York: National HomeCaring Council, 1983.

Norris, Jane, ed. *Daughters of the Elderly: Building Partnerships in Caregiving*. Bloomington: Indiana University Press, 1988.

Pynoos, Jon, Evelyn Cohen, Claire Lucas, and Linda Davis. *Home Evaluation Checklist for the Elderly*. Los Angeles, Calif.: Long-Term Care Gerontology Center of UCLA/USC, 1986. (For copies, write to Assist, 8905 Fairview Road, Suite 300, Silver Spring, Md. 20910, or call (301) 589–6760.)

———. *Home Evaluation Resource Booklet for the Elderly*. Los Angeles, CA.: Long-Term Care Gerontology Center of UCLA/USC, 1986. (See previous entry for ordering information.)

Raper, Ann Trueblood, and Anne C. Kalicki, eds. *National Continuing Care Directory*. Des Plains, Ill.: Scott, Foresman, 1989. (Prepared for the American Association of Homes for the Aging.)

Salamon, M. J., and Gloria Rosenthal. *Home or Nursing Home: Making the Right Choices*. New York: Springer, 1990.

Salmen, John P. S. *The Do-Able Renewable Home: Making Your Home Fit Your Needs*. Washington, D.C.: AARP, 1985.

Satir, Virginia. *The New Peoplemaking*. Mountain View, CA.: Science and Behavior Books, 1988.

Scholen, Ken. *Home-Made Money: A Consumer's Guide to Home Equity Conversion*. 2d ed. Washington, D.C.: AARP, Consumer Affairs Program Department, 1990.

Shared Housing Resource Center. *Is Homesharing for You? A Self-Help Guide for Homeowners and Renters*. Philadelphia, Pa.: Shared Housing Resource Center, 1983.

———. *National Directory of Shared Housing Programs for Older People*. Philadelphia, Pa.: Shared Housing Resource Center, 1983.

Silverstone, Barbara, and H. K. Hyman. *You and Your Aging Parent.* New York: Pantheon, 1983.

Sumichrast, Michael, Ronald G. Shafer, and Marilyn Sumichrast. *Planning Your Retirement Housing.* Glenview, Ill.: Scott, Foresman, 1984. (An AARP book.)

Tools for Independent Living and Designs for Independent Living. 1986. (For copies write to Appliance Information Service, Whirlpool Corporation, Benton Harbor, MI 49022.)

Tools for Living. (For copies, write to 400 West Hunter Avenue, Maywood, NJ 07631.)

Urban Land Institute. *Housing for a Maturing Population.* Washington, D.C.: Urban Land Institute, 1988.

U.S. Consumer Product Safety Commission. *Safety for Older Consumers: Home Safety Checklist.* (A free copy is available by writing to Office of Information and Public Affairs, U.S. Consumer Product Safety Commission, Washington, D.C. 20207, or by calling 1-800-638-2772.)

U.S. Department of Health and Human Services. *Where to Turn for Help for Older Persons: A Guide for Action on Behalf of an Older Person.* Washington, D.C.: U.S. Department of Health and Human Services, Office of Human Development Services, Administration on Aging, 1987.

Ways and Means. (For copies write to 28001 Citrin Drive, Romulus, MI 48174.)

Appendix C

Aging Services Available to Older Americans and Their Caregivers*

Area Agencies on Aging administer and support a wide range of community-based supportive and nutrition services. Because local needs differ, not all elder care services function in the same manner or are necessarily available in every community. Services coordinated by Area Agencies on Aging include access services, community-based services, in-home services, and services to residents in facilities that provide institutional long-term care. A listing of commonly available services is provided below.

Access Services

Assisting older Americans and their caregivers with obtaining available services.

CLIENT ASSESSMENT. Administering examinations, procedures or tests to determine a client's need and/or eligibility for services. Information collected may include health status, financial status, daily living status, etc. Includes pre-nursing home admissions screening, as well as routine health screening (blood pressure, hearing, vision, diabetes) and testing.

CARE MANAGEMENT. Review and analysis of evidence or facts concerning an individual's social, psychological, and physical health problem(s). Commonly performed to make a conclusive statement about the

*Excerpted from *Directory of State and Area Agencies on Aging*, 1989–1990. Reprinted with permission of National Association of Area Agencies on Aging.

level of functional ability (i.e., mildly impaired, moderately impaired, severely impaired) and requisite support services needed. Usually results in a plan of care for services or assistance either in the form of a service plan or a treatment plan.

INFORMATION AND REFERRAL. Includes the provision of information to an individual about available public and voluntary services or resources and linkage to ensure the service will be delivered to the client. Also includes contact with the provider and/or caregivers on an individual's behalf.

TRANSPORTATION. Taking an individual from one location to another by public or personal vehicle. This may include ride-on buses or vans, or personal vehicles operated by volunteers.

Community-Based Services

Direct services available on a community level for all older Americans.

ADULT DAY CARE. A community-based group program designed to meet the needs of functionally impaired adults through an individual plan of care. It is a structured, comprehensive program that provides a variety of health, social, and related support services in a protective setting during any part of the day, but less than 24-hour care. Individuals who participate in adult day care attend on a planned basis during specified hours. Their programs vary, but services usually include counseling and health assessments, health education, personal care, therapies, nutritious midday meals, social activities, and transportation to and from the center and transportation for special outings and doctors' appointments.

CONGREGATE MEALS. Hot or cold meals that assure a minimum of one-third of the Required Daily Allowance (RDA) to a group of older persons at a group facility. Congregate meals may be made available at senior centers, schools, churches, or other sites.

LEGAL ASSISTANCE. Many communities offer legal services. For those elderly who are unable to appropriately manage their own affairs, legal and/or protective services may be needed. Such services are designed to safeguard the rights and interests of older persons, to protect them from harm, to protect their property, and to provide advice and counsel to older persons and their families in dealing with financial and business concerns. Some legal issues that older persons and their families may be interested in could include: power of attorney; guardianship; wills; "right to die" living wills; government benefits and entitlements; consumer services; landlord/tenant problems; pensions; age discrimination; family law; etc.

SENIOR CENTER PROGRAMS. Across the country, there are more than twelve thousand senior centers supporting group activities for social, physical, religious, and recreational purposes. In many communities, multipurpose senior centers (MPSC) function as a focal point for comprehensive service delivery. An MPSC provides a social environment coordinating health and social services and designing adult education programs. Many centers function as meal sites and cultural centers and as such are an important vehicle for reaching the "underserved" elderly.

ELDER ABUSE PREVENTION PROGRAMS. Refers to various state and community programs such as adult protection and guardianship/conservatorship designed to alleviate situations of abuse, neglect, or self-neglect. Examples of such maltreatment could include physical abuse, psychological abuse, material abuse (theft or misuse of property), and medical abuse. All states and many local communities have an ombudsman responsible for investigating and resolving complaints made by or on behalf of residents of long-term care facilities.

EMPLOYMENT SERVICES. May include such service components as client assessment as a basis for developing a plan for securing employment; testing; job counseling and preretirement counseling; education and training; job development and job placement.

In-Home Services

Direct services to older Americans in their homes. Designed to assist individuals stay in their homes and with their families as long as possible.

HOME-DELIVERED MEALS. Often called "Meals-On-Wheels," can be delivered five or more days a week to individuals unable to shop and prepare food on their own. These services provide enhanced nutrition and a sense of security for the homebound elderly.

HOME HEALTH SERVICES. Covers many services often under a nurse's or doctor's supervision. These may include skilled nursing care, health monitoring and evaluation, dispensing medication, physical and other types of therapy, psychological counseling, and instructing individuals or families about ongoing care.

HOMEMAKER. Assist individuals with many of the tasks essential to maintaining a household, from food shopping and preparing meals to light housekeeping and laundry.

CHORE SERVICES. Goes beyond homemaking to include more heavy-duty tasks, such as floor or window washing, minor home repairs, yardwork, and other types of home maintenance.

TELEPHONE REASSURANCE. Provided by some agencies or volunteer organizations through regular prescheduled calls to the homebound. Ensuring personal safety is the main objective of these programs, but calls also reduce social isolation by providing personal phone contact with homebound individuals.

FRIENDLY VISITING. A volunteer program of periodic neighborly visits to homebound elders for the purpose of providing social contact, interaction, and reassurance.

ENERGY ASSISTANCE AND WEATHERIZATION. Low-income home energy and weatherization assistance is available in most states to help eligible families in paying their fuel bills or weatherizing their homes (insulation, caulking, storm windows, etc.)

Appendix D

Children of Aging Parents (CAPS)

Children of Aging Parents (CAPS) is a national organization open to all individuals, professionals, and organizations who have an interest in caregiving for the elderly. It is dedicated to increasing community awareness of the problems of aging and caregiving through education programs, workshops, support groups, and seminars and serves as a clearinghouse for individuals and organizations serving families with aging parents or relatives. CAPS also publishes a national newsletter, *The Capsule,* that provides advice and current information to caregivers. Its many services and programs include the following:

- Nationwide informational and referral services for caregivers
- Production and distribution of literature for caregivers
- Individual peer counseling services for caregivers through support groups or by telephone
- Employee assistance programs

CAPS is a nonprofit 501-C3 organization. All donations and memberships are tax deductible. Individuals interested in more information concerning CAPS should send a self-addressed, stamped envelope to the following address:

> Children of Aging Parents
> 1609 Woodbourne Road, 302A
> Levitown, PA 19057
> (215) 945–6900

Appendix E

Family Service America, Inc. (FSA)

Founded in 1911, Family Service America, Inc. (FSA) is a network of 290 local agencies throughout the United States and Canada. The membership includes accredited nonsectarian and sectarian organizations. FSA is staffed by well-trained professionals and is the foremost source of professional counseling programs and other services directed toward the strengthening of families.

FSA member agencies are nonprofit organizations governed by volunteer citizens from their communities. Agencies receive income from a variety of sources, including local United Ways and other fund-raising groups.

One of FSA's many programs is service to assist individuals and families to solve problems associated with increased family pressures related to aging parents. These services include:

1. Support groups for caregivers to elderly parents and spouses.
2. Assessment and case management.
3. Individual and family counseling for persons involved in caregiving.
4. Information and referral.
5. Homemaker services.
6. Friendly visitor services.

For information on your nearest FSA, call or write to:

Family Service America, Inc.
11700 West Lake Park Drive
Milwaukee, Wisconsin 53224
(414) 359-1040

Appendix F

What Is a "Private Geriatric Care Manager"?

The private geriatric care manager is a professional with a graduate degree in the field of human services (social work, psychology, gerontology) or its substantial equivalent (e.g., R.N.), certified or licensed at the independent practice level of his or her profession, who is duly trained and experienced in the assessment, coordination, monitoring, and direct delivery of services to the elderly and their families.

Services provided by private geriatric care managers may include some or all of the following:

- Assessment
- Counseling
- Assessment, implementation, and long-term monitoring of home care
- Crisis intervention
- Placement
- Care management
- Entitlements
- Advocacy
- Psychotherapy
- Education
- Consultation
- Information and referral

The private geriatric care manager receives referrals from families (especially those living at a distance from their elders), from attorneys, hospitals, physicians, trust departments of banks, conservators, community agencies, employee assistance programs, and the general public.

Address:
655 North Alvernon Way
Suite 108
Tuscon, AZ 85711

Notes

Introduction

1. *Understanding Senior Housing for the 1990s, An AARP Survey of Consumer, Preferences, Concerns, and Needs.* (Washington, D.C.: AARP), 1990.
2. *A Profile of Older Americans,* (Washington, D.C.: AARP and Administration on Aging, U.S. Department of Health and Human Services, 1990), 1.
3. Elaine M. Brody, "Caregiving Crisis in the Family" (lecture for Jewish Family Service of the Delaware Valley, Trenton, N.J., 11 May 1988).
4. Larry Hugick, "Women Play the Leading Role in Keeping Modern Families Close," *The Gallup Poll News Service,* 54, no. 9 (July 3, 1989).
5. Amy Horowitz, "Sons and Daughters as Caregivers to Older Persons," *The Gerontologist* 25, no.6 (1985).
6. Hugick, 1989.

Chapter 1. Should Mom Live With Us?

1. Alex Comfort, *Practice of Geriatric Psychiatry.* (New York: Elsevier, 1980).

Chapter 2. Can Mom Manage in Her Own Home?

1. Adapted from Ken Scholen, *Home-Made Money: A Consumer's Guide to Home Equity Conversion* (Washington, D.C.: AARP, 1990), 7-9. Reprinted with permission.
2. Ibid., 10.
3. Ibid., 20.
4. Ibid., 25, 26.
5. Ibid., 32, 33.
6. Material obtained from Tom Ostrowski, Mortgage Loan Office, Virginia Home Equity Program, Virginia Housing Development Authority, 1989.
7. Scholen, 1990, 34, 37.
8. Judith V. May, "Home Equity Conversion Mortgage Insurance Demonstration Program Briefing Paper" (Washington, D.C.: Office of Policy Development and Research, HUD, September 1989).

9. Ibid.
10. Robert Sunley, "Home Sharing," *Proceedings—New Options for Living: Expanding Housing Choices for the Elderly* (Trenton, NJ: New Jersey Department of Community Affairs, Division on Aging, September 1980), 119–24.

Chapter 3. Can Mom's Home Be Made Safe and Secure?

1. John A. Krout, "Area Agencies on Aging Planning and Service Provision for the Rural Elderly," Final Report to the Retirement Research Foundation (Fredonia, N.Y.: SUNY, Fredonia, August 1989).
2. "Products and Services," *Spectrum,* March–April 1989, 25.
3. Ibid.
4. Lorraine G. Hiatt, "Understanding the Physical Environment," *Pride Institute Journal of Long-Term Care* 4, no.2 (1985): 15.
5. Ibid.
6. "Senior Citizens Security Housing and Transportation Program," (Trenton, N.J.: New Jersey Department of Community Affairs, Division on Aging, 1988).
7. Paper written by Donald L. Moon, president, Jeanes/Foulkeways Corporation, Philadelphia, Pa., 1989.

Chapter 5. Can Parent and Child Live Together?

1. Ken Dychtwald, *Age Wave* (New York: Bantam Books, 1990).
2. R. J. Havighurst and Kenneth Feigenbaum, "Leisure and Lifestyle," in *Middle Age and Aging,* ed. Bernice Neugarten et al. (Chicago: University of Chicago Press, 1975), 348.
3. Ibid.
4. Erik Erikson, Joan Erikson and Helen Kirnick, *Vital Involvement in Old Age* (New York: W. W. Norton, 1986).
5. B. L. Neugarten, R. J. Havighurst and S. S. Tob, "Personality and Patterns of Aging," 1975 in *Middle Age and Aging,* ed. Bernice Neugarten et al. (Chicago: University of Chicago Press, 1975), 76.
6. James Lynch, *The Language of the Heart: The Body's Response to Human Dialogue* (New York: Basic Books, 1986).
7. Elaine M. Brody, "All Generations Need the Gift of Caring," *National Association of Social Workers News,* March 1986.

Chapter 6. Negotiating a Living Together Agreement

1. "Nursing Homes in the Future," *New York Times,* 28 February 1991, B15, cols. 5, 6.

Chapter 7. Ensuring Safety and Privacy in the Child's Home

1. *National Council on Aging Newsletter,* January 1991. We also recommend the pamphlet "Keep It Safe at Home, on the Road," which is obtainable at no charge by sending a stamped, self-addressed, business envelope with your request to Keep It Safe, P.O. Box 3717, Washington, D.C., 20007.
2. Helen Franklin, "The 1988 Tech Act: Aids to Independent Living Get Nod from Congress," *The Aging Connection,* August–September 1990, 12.

Chapter 8. How to Keep the Harmony

1. Mark Edinberg, *Talking with Your Aging Parents* (Boston: Shambhala, 1988).
2. Virginia Satir, *The New PeopleMaking* (Mountainview, Calif.: Science and Behavior Books, 1988).
3. James Lynch, *The Language of the Heart: The Body's Response to Human Dialogue* (New York: Basic Books, 1986).
4. Lee Headley, *Adults and Their Parents in Family Therapy* (New York: Plenum Press, 1977).
5. Robert Butler, "The Life Review: An Interpretation of Reminiscence in the Aged," in *Middle Age and Aging,* ed. Bernice Neugarten et al., (Chicago: University of Chicago Press, 1975).
6. Headley, 1977.

Chapter 9. Support From the Outside

1. Ruth Van Behren, "Adult Day Care: A Decade of Growth," *Prospective on Aging,* July–August 1989, 14.
2. Susan C. Ficke, ed, *An Orientation to the Older Americans Act* (Washington, D.C.: National Association of State Units on Aging, July 1985), 53.
3. "Employers and Eldercare," *Working Age* (AARP Newsletter) 4, no. 6 (May–June 1989): 3.

Chapter 10. His Mother, Not Hers

1. Amy Horowitz, "Sons and Daughters as Caregivers to Older Parents," *The Gerontologist* 25, no.6 (1985): 615.
2. Elaine M. Brody, *Women in the Middle: Their Parent Care Years* (New York: Springer, 1990).
3. Ibid., 185.
4. Ibid., 44.

Chapter 11. From Our Home to Nursing Home

1. Elaine M. Brody, *Women in the Middle: Their Parent Care Years* (New York: Springer, 1990).
2. M. J. Salamon and Gloria Rosenthal, *Home or Nursing Home: Making the Right Choice* (New York: Springer, 1990).
3. N. R. Hooyman, *Taking Care: Supporting Older People and Their Families* (New York: Free Press, 1986).
4. Salamon and Rosenthal, 1990, 44.

Chapter 12. Future Possibilities

1. Ken Dychtwald, *Age Wave* (New York: Bantam Books, 1990), 251.
2. Charles H. Mindel, "Multigenerational Family Households: Recent Trends and Implications for the Future," *The Gerontologist* 19, no.5 (1979): 461–62.
3. Elaine M. Brody, "Caregiving Crisis in the Family" (lecture at the Jewish Family Service of the Delaware Valley, Trenton, N.J., 11 May 1988).
4. *Elder Care Referral Service* (Armonk, N.Y.: IBM, 1988), 1.
5. May Engler, et al., "Partnership for Elder Care: A Service Model for the Future" (paper presented at the Forty-Third Annual Meeting of the Gerontological Society of America, Boston, Mass., November 1990).
6. May Engler, et al. "Partnership for Eldercare: A Service Model for the Future." (Paper presented at the 43rd Annual Scientific Meeting of the Gerontogical Society of America, Boston, Mass., November 1990), 6.
7. Dychtwald, 1990, 251.
8. Kathryn McComant and Charles Durrett, *Cohousing: A Contemporary Approach to Housing Ourselves* (Berkeley, Calif.: Habitat Press, 1989), 142.
9. U.S. Senator Bill Bradley's proposed bill entitled: *Summary of Provisions: Family Caregiver Support Act of 1991.*

Acknowledgments

We thank, first and foremost, the hundreds of caregivers and their families who, over the years, have shared with us their struggles and taught us so much about caregiving. Next, we wish to thank the staff and participants of the many housing and community programs and social agencies who gave so generously of their time.

In addition, personal thanks to family, friends, and others who willingly shared their experiences with us. Their help was indispensible. We hope this book will serve our readers well as a guide to making wise living arrangement decisions.

Extra thanks to Terri Baker who did the special typing for us.

Index

About the
Authors

Vivian F. Carlin received a Ph.D. in social policy and gerontology from Rutgers University. Also a certified psychologist, Dr. Carlin is a consulting gerontologist who specializes in housing and preretirement planning. She is the coauthor of *If I Live to be 100 . . . A Creative Housing Solution for Older People,* and *Where Can Mom Live? A Family Guide to Living Arrangements for Older Parents* and the author of *Can Mom Live Alone? Practical Advice on Helping Aging Parents Stay in Their Own Home.* Dr. Carlin retired from her position as supervisor of the Office of Planning and Policy Analysis of the New Jersey State Division on Aging. On the division staff for fifteen years, she developed such new programs as Elderly Home Conversion (the first in the United States) and Congregate Housing Services (the first in New Jersey and third in the nation). She has presented papers and led training sessions at regional, national, and international gerontology conferences, and has appeared as a guest on a number of radio and TV shows.

Vivian E. Greenberg, M.S.S., A.C.S.W., is a graduate of Bryn Mawr College, the Graduate School of Social Work and Social Research. She also holds degrees from Douglass College and Columbia University. Her first book, *Your Best Is Good Enough,* was published in 1989. Currently, she is in private practice in Pennington, New Jersey. Prior to this she was a clinical specialist in gerontological social work with Jewish Family Service of the Delaware Valley, Trenton, New Jersey and was associate director of geriatric education of the Family Medicine Residency Program of Memorial Hospital of Burlington County, Mount Holly, New Jersey. She has extensive experience leading counseling groups for caregivers and teaching geriatrics to those in related health care fields.